SHERIFF MIKE LEWIS

Dave,

Thanks for your Continual Support.

Wishing you and your family

Abundant Joy and Success.

Michael D. Lewis

3/8/22

ISBN-13: 978-1-955937-46-7 (Paperback)

ISBN-13: 978-1-955937-02-3 (eBook)

Published by Defiance Press and Publishing, LLC

Bulk orders of this book may be obtained by contacting Defiance Press and Publishing, LLC. www.defiancepress.com.

Defiance Press & Publishing, LLC

281-581-9300 info@defiancepress.com

SHERIFF MIKE LEWIS

CONSTITUTIONAL.
UNCANCELED.

By Haven P. Simmons, Ph.D.

Dedicated to America's first responders

TABLE OF CONTENTS

CHAPTER ONE

FORMATIVE INFLUENCES AND DRUG

INTERDICTION

The Eastern Shore of Maryland is sometimes considered an afterthought with limited relevance to one of the most densely populated, oddly configured, and geographically petite states in America—probably the reason natives of the aberrant location castigate the FBIs (F-ing Baltimore Idiots) and Baltimorons. They rebuff the historically unflattering perceptions among legislators in Annapolis, where a former governor labeled the Eastern Shore the "outhouse" of Maryland. These detractors are considered insufferable snobs, given the obvious irony and provinciality in such sentiments. After all, Talbot is the richest county in the state per capita, and Ocean City attracts hundreds of thousands of tourists with sand in their shoes from "Western Shore" Baltimore and its adjacent suburbs. The Eastern Shore, decidedly torn between North and South during the Civil War, is "flatter than a fritter" in parochial parlance, a section of the Delmarva Peninsula entailing Delaware, an awkward chunk of Maryland, and a narrow strip of Virginia dividing the Chesapeake Bay and the Atlantic Ocean. Its topography showcases meandering waterways and loblolly pine trees. Certain inhabitants of the region have argued it should secede as a separate state, cutting ties with Maryland and Virginia. The hub of the Eastern Shore is racially diverse, and with a population exceeding 100,000, Wicomico County is located just below the Mason-Dixon Line, approximately two and one-half hours from Baltimore, Washington, D.C., Philadelphia, and southernmost Virginia Beach that connects Florida to New York along U.S. 13. The area is far more agricultural than many people realize, growing wheat, corn, and vegetables, with a bustling poultry industry. Freight trains are heard night and day pushing through the middle of (county seat) Salisbury, the "crossroads" of the peninsula, at predictable pitch and cadence. The Eastern Shore also claims a legacy of rugged crabbers and fishermen, some of whom plied their trade living on the remote Tangier and Smith Islands. Wallops Island is home to an extensive NASA facility, not far from Chincoteague, where wild ponies roam the national seashore each year. The frenetic Western Shore pace changes when motorists, having crossed the Chesapeake Bay Bridge with its spectacular views, turn south after driving through Kent Island on their way to Easton, Cambridge, Salisbury, and Ocean City. There is a reassuring sense of relief and calm as traffic diminishes, especially out of season, and the highway traverses a rural setting of farms and small towns escaping the congestion and madness of the Western Shore. The U.S. 50 bypass around Salisbury a relatively seamless path to Ocean City, doesn't supplant the Eastern Shore's premiere hospital, corporate titan Perdue Farms, Salisbury University and Wor-Wic Community College, a significant zoo relative to the size of the community, the Delmarva

Shorebirds minor league baseball team, two network television affiliates, the world-famous Ward Museum featuring wildfowl carvings, or the pre-eminence of Wicomico County Sheriff Mike Lewis, one of the nation's most influential law enforcement figures.

Sheriff Lewis is "constitutionally correct" in a traditional Republican stronghold once considered distant and inconsequential amid Maryland's reputation as an overwhelmingly blue state.

He challenges onerous, politically correct national narratives impugning law enforcement, the greater society, and the country. Passionate. Persistent. Pugnacious. Exuberance that leaves people wondering whether he sleeps at night. A sturdy, compact man donning his trademark ten-gallon Stetson hat over a classic crew cut for photo ops with sheriff's personnel and equipment. He juxtaposes a stridently confident demeanor with a friendly countenance and polite greetings. But his public speaking skills particularly impress with rapid urgency and intonation that rivet colleagues, members of the media, and the general public, including college students who abandon their beloved cell phones to listen intently for two hours at a time. His ability to personally extol and converse with gatherings of constituents is legend. Rare critics find him controversial but seemingly appreciate his uncanny knack for engaging the audience, many of whom have voted for the gregarious sheriff in four consecutive elections.

"He is one of the most well-read men I have ever met. He could tell you what the Federalist Papers say about many topics. He is a deep thinker and an incredible writer and orator, one of the best; one certainly does not want to follow Sheriff Lewis in giving a speech to any crowd of people," said Wicomico Circuit Court Judge Matt

Maciarello, who interacted with him while prosecuting criminal cases as state's attorney.

In popular culture policing, Lewis transcends affable, prudent small town sheriff Andy Taylor of idyllic Mayberry, North Carolina, and constitutional but no-nonsense Matt Dillon's determination to "clean up Dodge" as U.S. Marshal.

Fittingly, a few years ago, the sheriff was in Mount Airy, North Carolina, relishing the Andy Griffith Museum. "A woman came up and asked me what I was doing down there," Lewis recalled. "She said she knew I was the sheriff from Maryland she had seen on TV."

Lewis's background and proclivities have manifested in the small Western town his dad built on rural Wicomico County property—a wooden boardwalk, saloon, and jailhouse displaying posters of heroic sheriffs from the movies and wanted outlaws.

The jurisdiction he and the sheriff's office preside over was named after the Wicomico Native people who Captain John Smith first encountered in the early 1600s. Encroachment and manipulation displaced the tribe to a reservation south of the Great Wicomico River, a Chesapeake Bay tributary. The bay was created by a meteor that collided with earth, and the subsequent melting of glaciers.

No one confuses the vigorous sheriff's impact with that of a meteor, but his ascent to becoming a household name in Wicomico County and beyond might be called meteoric. "There is nothing like it. I have traveled the world speaking and training. We don't pretend to be something we're not," he said pridefully about his Eastern Shore roots. "Your level of education and what you do for a living doesn't matter. It is a very friendly place."

4

That vibe was evident at lunch when, on break from our initial interview for this book, the author witnessed his amicable exchanges with patrons at the Pecan Square deli several blocks from the sheriff's office. Sitting in the back with a lieutenant and this scribe provided some semblance of privacy and the safety habitually sought in public by law enforcement officers, but Lewis ended up speaking to nearly all of the dozen diners, gladly accepting an elderly man's invitation to address VFW members in the coming weeks. Rather than looking dubiously at the sheriff as if he were from planet Mars, as many people do when they see uniformed police, the patrons' familiarity and ease implied the intimacy of the community where Lewis had grown up.

In addition to diligently wearing a mask, the self-professed "hugger" usually resists the temptation to wrap his arms around friends. "My deputies remind me not to do that with the COVID-19 outbreak," said the sheriff, who was recently swarmed by customers wanting pictures taken with him at a preferred haunt on Main Street.

The owner of Kellyn's Kafe, Andrew Hanna, said two elderly women were enamored that day with the customized semi-automatic handgun Sheriff Lewis wore on his hip.

He bought the .45 caliber Kimber super-carry custom "911" weapon on his own dime after becoming sheriff. The model renders World War One and World War Two legacies and, Lewis said, "screams *made in America*." Through the connections of a fellow sheriff in Texas, the grips are adorned with State of Maryland and Wicomico County Sheriff's Office emblems made out of silver, gold, and pewter made by a prison inmate serving life for first-degree murder.

The night before our interview, he drove to the small town of

Powellville after learning an old friend named "Uncle Sonny" had died. Sheriff Lewis helped the caretakers lift him into a body bag. The deceased was married to "Aunt Sweetie Pie," and they were distant relatives of Lewis's spouse.

The death capped a fourteen-hour day for Sheriff Lewis starting when a deputy's mother was involved in a car crash on Route 113, which angles from Pocomoke, Maryland, to Delaware. Tree trimmers assisted the woman to the side of the road where, as she was trying to gather her composure, another vehicle ran over and killed her. Sorrow reverberated around the Wicomico County Sheriff's Office as Lewis and his deputies commiserated over the loss.

"He was a precious kid. I loved that boy. I absolutely loved him," Lewis said when Fruitland police officer Spencer Wiersberg perished from bone cancer at the age of twenty-one. Wiersberg was the son of Wicomico County Sheriff's Lieutenant Rich Wiersberg. The Lewis and Wiersberg families were close, often enjoying Baltimore Ravens games and other outings together.

Spencer Wiersberg, a graduate of the Easter Shore Law Enforcement Academy, amassed an exceptional number of arrests and citations over his fleeting but acclaimed career. The community coalesced to raise money for his struggle against the dreaded disease. Sheriff Lewis befriended Spencer when he was ten.

Maryland Senator Mary Beth Carozza has never forgotten Lewis's unrelenting attentiveness following the suicide of her brother, a Wicomico County assistant public defender. She said Lewis was a "rock of support over the years," devoting time to "check up on us with a funny story or memory of all the good Tony had done not only in his job, but as a friend, son, father, husband, and of course, brother."

"He is the friendly neighborhood sheriff that knows everyone's name, knows how their kids are doing in school. Mike has an amazing ability to make someone feel appreciated," enthused Rick Pollitt, a Salisbury *Daily Times* reporter, and former seasonal police officer in Ocean City, whose grandfather was Wicomico County sheriff for twelve years.

Lewis developed an interest in law enforcement while lamenting high school "friends and associates" who were heading in the wrong direction doing drugs. "I knew the drugs were coming in here," he explained. "I wanted to do something about it."

Indeed, law enforcement is in his blood—as demonstrated by myriad, telling memories. When Lewis was only four years old, for instance, his father, also a deputy, responded to the fatal shootings of Sheriff Sam Graham and a corrections officer by a self-professed heroin addict whose girlfriend smuggled a gun into the county jail in a box of candy. "I can see (my dad) driving away in a white patrol unit with the small sheriff's logo on the side," Lewis said.

The killer died several years ago in prison.

Michael A. Lewis was "born poor" on the east side of Salisbury as one of six children, three girls and three boys. He attended Powell elementary, now the VFW hall, and Beaver elementary, followed by Wicomico junior and senior high schools. His dad also worked as a self-employed contractor, and his mom was a cashier at Super Fresh for thirty-four years. Lewis learned to hunt and fish as a youngster, forming a passion for the sanctity of the outdoors and possessing firearms that persevere to this day. The family owned a home on Mount Hermon Road that had snakes crawling through holes in the drywall; it was eventually condemned and razed in a "training burn" by the fire department. Their next house was on Walston Switch Road.

As a teenager, the resourceful Lewis held jobs at Sammy and Johnny's restaurant, Food Market in the old Salisbury Mall, and Perdue Farms.

Lewis and five high school classmates had been processed through the "buddy" system to join the Marines, but Lewis reconsidered at an open house conducted by the Maryland State Police because being a trooper had been his ultimate goal anyway.

Lewis's faithful companion and biggest fan, of course, has been Denise. They dated for five years before tying the knot. She was an RN for twenty-eight years at the area's largest hospital, Peninsula Regional Medical Center, and remains in the health care field specializing in obstetrics.

Mike and Denise attend Emmanuel Wesleyan Church in Salisbury.

Adam, his thirty-year-old son, is the creative marketing director for a firm in Florida owned by two former Marines. "He says they remind him of me," the sheriff said with a smile.

Daughter Ally, twenty-five, is a teacher in Virginia and engaged to be married.

Both children graduated from Salisbury University.

"It starts with his family," Maciarello said. "He is deeply committed to his family and close friends. I would say 80% of any day, Sheriff Lewis is giving to others, helping someone else. Few individuals other than maybe local clergy, gave that much of themselves."

While never shirking his responsibility to serve the community (and never tiring of adrenaline-drenched chases), a more relaxed high-performance avocation for Lewis is motorcycle riding. His office is embellished with black and orange Harley Davidson collector items.

Lewis became a trooper shortly after high school, navigating a decorated career as one of the most prolific drug interdiction officers ever. In fact, the Maryland State Police transferred him to the Western Shore when drug traffickers using the US 13 corridor between Florida and New York put a "bounty" on his head.

The plot surfaced from intelligence gathered by MSP supervisors. After three months of desk detail that almost drove him mad, he returned to the road when the threat dissipated.

Declining national crime rates in the 1990s accompanied concerns about "stop and frisk" measures, such as those implemented under Mayor Rudolph Giuliani in New York, and racial profiling that alleged minorities were unfairly targeted by law enforcement. The superintendent of the New Jersey State Police, for instance, was terminated after strongly linking blacks and Hispanics to drug crimes. Claims of racial profiling competed with police discretion that allows officers to evaluate suspects according to age, time of day, location, attire, body language, and other relevant factors.

"I learned a long time ago, when you're doing good police work and you're arresting bad guys and removing them from the streets, there will always be allegations of racial profiling," Lewis said. "Consequently, if your case is rock-solid, defense counsel will often times resort to playing the race card. It is the nature of the beast."

According to Tom Trinko of the *American Thinker*. "If a liberal dislikes the police because they think they are unfairly targeting his 'harmless' drug use it's not a big step for them to assume that cops are racist and 'violent' toward other 'innocent' people. If a liberal believes cops are 'racist pigs,' then it becomes clear that arresting 'innocent' drug users is an act of fascist repression and that drug dealers are actually the victims of a 'police state.'"

At the beginning, with the state police, a preponderance of Lewis's narcotics arrests involved "dirtball" whites on town thoroughfares and rural roads for possession. But when he started patrolling the major Eastern Shore arteries, US 13 and US 50, the dynamics changed. "I moved to the highway. I was taking off two or three kilograms of coke, instead of two or three grams. I was mostly locking up blacks. I couldn't help it," he said, admitting suspects occasionally labeled him a racist.

"I debriefed hundreds of black smugglers. I asked them why they didn't hire white guys (as decoys) to deliver the drugs, and they would laugh and say they couldn't trust them."

Horrific sadness besieged the Maryland State Police in the fall of 1995 when one of Lewis's fellow troopers, Kevin Plank, was shot fatally in the face by drug runners he had stopped for speeding shortly after midnight on US 13 close to his hometown of Princess Anne, ten miles south of Salisbury. The two suspects, one from New York and the other from North Carolina, were eventually apprehended. A pound of cocaine with a street value of $83,000 was found in the getaway car, detailed Lewis. A stretch of highway is named in Plank's honor.

The twenty-eight-year-old's demise hit close to home for Lewis, as they were both fathers of newborn children. Lewis tearfully lamented his death as the product of burgeoning drug trafficking on the somewhat sparse highway linking Virginia Beach and Norfolk in the Hampton Roads area to Philadelphia through the Eastern Shore. Drug dealers had determined that the route, with an ultimate north south expanse from New York to Florida, was more direct and less heavily patrolled than Interstate 95 dissecting the Washington, D.C./ Baltimore metro. Presumably plying a lucrative trade, they were indifferent to the hefty toll for the ten-mile Chesapeake Bay "tunnel" bridge connecting Virginia Beach to the Eastern Shore.

Two years before Plank died, he provided backup when Lewis pulled over an old Cadillac just south of Dagsboro Road on the southbound side. Unsurprisingly, the two occupants were from the Virginia Beach-Norfolk Hampton Roads area. They attempted to discourage the troopers from searching the vehicle by showing them traffic tickets received the same day in Harrington, Delaware, for equipment violations.

Lewis found over seven pounds of crack cocaine and a .45 handgun, the same caliber that ultimately claimed Trooper Plank's life, in a hidden fabricated compartment behind the back seat. A second weapon was retrieved from another compartment in the dashboard next to the steering wheel.

The driver and the passenger, both of whom had extensive criminal histories, were sentenced to forty-five and twenty-five years, respectively.

"I take great joy in seeing drug traffickers go to prison for lengthy periods of time—absolutely. They should go away for a long time. We all have a friend, a relative, a neighbor that's suffering from addiction."

Around that juncture, troopers on the Eastern Shore also scored what was then the second-largest seizure of methamphetamine on a Maryland highway.

Suspicion and probable cause preceding traffic stops originate from erratic driving, sketchy identification, conflicting stories, nervousness, and in a case involving two suspects arrested on US 13, seventy-two air fresheners hanging on the rearview mirror to mitigate the odor of narcotics.

In January of 1996, at the age of thirty-one, Corporal Lewis would tempt a similar fate as his Maryland State Police compatriot on US 13. Patrolling the bypass near Salisbury, he observed a speeding gold Lexus displaying North Carolina plates that erratically cut in front of another vehicle. After pulling the car over, Lewis said he detected the smell of weed and discovered marijuana when the driver granted him permission to search the car. While attempting to arrest the suspect, a scuffle ensued, and the man unsuccessfully attempted to pilfer Lewis's service revolver. The assailant then led him on a foot chase through a nearby housing development. Somehow, the individual circled back to the car, jumped in, and tried to run over the approaching trooper. Lewis fired several shots at the vehicle and its lone occupant in self-defense. A trucker who witnessed the altercation drove ahead and parked his eighteen-wheeler across the US 13 bypass, blocking the suspect's path.

It turned out that Keith Hill, a young man from Brooklyn, New York, had been shot in the upper torso. He died a short time later at the hospital. The search of the car uncovered $3,100 cash and fifty-eight grams of marijuana.

"I felt like I was going to die that day when I ran into traffic to get away from him," Lewis said. "The truck driver said he expected to see me caught in the axle."

Lewis said faith in the Lord Jesus Christ saved his life during the ordeal. "If I didn't have faith, I couldn't put on that uniform and walk out the door every day. The Lord has provided my family, the equipment to do my job, faith in my employer, the people I work with, and my fellow man."

According to the sheriff, he did not suffer PTSD (Post Traumatic Stress Disorder) from the experience. "I was angry that he tried to kill me. I was angry I had to kill him."

He did, however, "think about it every day" for years, "especially when I activated the blue lights to stop someone and thinking this could be my time to die out on the roadway."

"I knew I had taken the life of a man who was someone's son, someone's brother, someone's father," he said ruefully.

Keith Hill was, indeed, a father whose son began communicating with Sheriff Lewis on January 26, 2020, the twenty-fourth anniversary of his dad's demise and the day that basketball legend Kobe Bryant died in a helicopter crash. Lewis said the combination of dates and numbers was strikingly symbolic. The son is a huge fan of Bryant, who wore numbers eight and twenty-four during his career. Furthermore, this scribe's second interview with the sheriff was in his office on

January 26, 2021, twenty-five years to the day since the shooting.

"He (the son) says he harbors no ill will toward me and he wants to stay in touch," Lewis said. "He asked about me maybe meeting his family one day."

Lewis has counseled officers around the country who killed someone in the line of duty. "I oftentimes thank them for having the courage to pull the trigger. Because if they don't pull the trigger, they could be a statistic or an innocent civilian could be a statistic."

The specter of shooting an "unarmed black man" loomed for Corporal Lewis, but he was cleared of wrongdoing in the case by criminal and internal investigations. Lewis said a "super-charged" belief in the Constitution he still holds today has always obligated him to focus on the seriousness of the crime, veracity of the evidence, and the demeanor and possible criminal history of the individual, superseding color in making arrests.

Lewis was suspended from his position without pay following the Hill shooting. His first day back on the road brought more drama when he attempted to stop a speeding southbound car on US 13, precipitating a two-county chase reaching 115 miles per hour. It ended at a roadblock as the suspect tossed bags of cocaine out of his car.

A highlight for Lewis was seeing photos displayed at the capitol building in Annapolis of the elite trooper squad he created and managed. Governor Robert Ehrlich personally awarded the members plaques for intercepting drug traffickers and contraband on I-95 following his redeployment to the Western Shore.

Lewis said some law enforcement officers are less prone to suspect women for being actively involved in the drug trade, but that they often function as accessories to crime, at the very least. He recalled one of the troopers he supervised, Jack Cameron, stopping a female driver on I-95 who appeared to be unduly nervous. Closer scrutiny revealed two bullet-riddled, bound and gagged bodies in the trunk of the car, a narcotics concealment compartment, and $106,000 cash.

The general public, elaborated Lewis, is not aware that drug operatives historically employ "caravans" of vehicles with escorts and decoys that are known to distract law enforcement from a car that has been detained by committing multiple traffic violations.

"There was no formal training back then, and very few troopers experienced measurable success. I'm proud to say, the criminal profiles we developed are now customarily used throughout the nation in the apprehension of terrorists, bombers, murder suspects, and have resulted in seizures of millions of dollars of drugs and U.S. currency."

"I didn't want to leave the state police," said Lewis, who retired at the rank of sergeant. "I had a fabulous career," one that instigated demand for his knowledge of drug interdiction in training law enforcement personnel from the United States, Great Britain, Australia, the West Indies, and Russia, and numerous seminars about how to conduct the safest, most efficient traffic stops."

But when five-term Wicomico County Sheriff Hunter Nelms announced he was not going for re-election, Lewis rationalized it was "now or never" to run for the position; running as a Republican, he soon emerged victorious from a field of seven candidates. Signature campaign platforms addressing civic organizations, neighborhood associations, forums, and the media were the merits of aggressive, advanced measures for mitigating the narcotics trade, which spurs an array of crimes in the community, and modernizing the sheriff's office. He espoused to "stand up" for the law enforcement's core values of courage, honor, and integrity that were adopted at the Wicomico County Sheriff's Office upon election to his fledgling fouryear term.

"First impressions are lasting, and Mike immediately demonstrated an aura of confidence and purpose," said Wicomico County Councilman John Cannon, who initially sought office the same year as Lewis. "Mike had that 'take charge' persona upon entering a room or the stage."

John Sharpe's stepfather, who served honorably in World War Two, raved about a drug eradication presentation by Lewis during his first campaign. "I met the sheriff at a neighborhood block party," Sharpe said. "He is a man of honesty. He is a man of integrity. He is a man of faith. He is a great sheriff."

When asked what makes his boss unique, Lieutenant Tim Robinson said: "His drive. His energy. His motivation. His organizational skills. When (Mike) first ran for office, I had a resident tell me how impressed he was with his message that he would not let politics interfere with his goal to rid Wicomico County of the criminal element. He resonated with the people."

Lewis participated in seven debates during the campaign. Opponents claimed he lacked administrative and budgetary background, which was largely true, but Lewis retorted that he would hire experts in those spheres. "I had chances to seek promotions toward administration and higher ranks the last eleven years with the

Maryland State Police but wanted to stay on the road as a trooper."

He promised to lead his office "from the trenches on the street."

He maintained his vow not to employ a complement of pals from the Maryland State Police at the sheriff's office. Lewis repelled concerns that he would be "part-time," fulfilling speaking and training commitments by affirming his belief in educating less experienced law enforcement officers without compromising the obligations of sheriff, simultaneously elevating the reputation of the Wicomico County Sheriff's office regionally and nationally.

Shortly after his election, deputies seized $105,000 from a drug runner's car that had been stopped along the US 50 bypass. Lewis said the money was found in a small remote-controlled dashboard, and a K-9 detected the smell of narcotics in the vehicle. By the time the investigation was complete, four pounds of marijuana and four flat-screen televisions were retrieved from the Princess Anne residence of a University of Maryland-Eastern Shore student who had been driving northbound toward New York.

It signaled a pattern of using money from drug seizures to purchase equipment for the sheriff's office at Lewis's direction, a nice addendum when he approached the county council for budget increases over the years. The $105,000 enabled the agency to obtain several patrol cars displaying placards boasting they were purchased with funds confiscated in the apprehension of drug runners.

"People have asked me why we don't just let the drug traffickers drive through Wicomico County back and forth to other destinations," Lewis said. "No one has a constitutional right to escape detection, so we continue to enforce the law when people pass through. They won't build their empire and retirement here."

In that light, Wicomico County is the only place on the Eastern Shore with HIDTA (High-Density Drug Trafficking Area) designation that qualifies for federal money. Lewis said the Wicomico County Sheriff's Office validated need through documented cases, some of which he worked as a state trooper.

Lewis admits that winning the war on drugs is virtually impossible. The United States, despite having 7% of the world's population, consumes more than two-thirds of the world's illicit drugs, owing to prosperity, Lewis said, but that doesn't mean law enforcement should abdicate its responsibility to enforce the laws against the scourge that contributes to addiction, mental instability, a plethora of social problems, and crime. Few offenders are rehabilitated in prison, he noted, resuming their criminality as parolees.

High-ranking personnel from the Royal Canadian Mounted Police and the Indianapolis Police Department joined Lewis early on as panelists for a drug interdiction video produced by Multijurisdictional Counterdrug Task Force Training (MCTFT).

Relating some of his front-line experience on the road as a trooper, Lewis said patrol officers should be cognizant of telltale indicators that narcotics are present in a vehicle, such as fabric softeners, duct tape, and brand-new tools for accessing hidden compartments. In some cases, airbags are removed to provide space for drugs.

In the piece, he said Atlanta was becoming the largest "hub" of narcotics in America and that tighter security in airports post-9/11 forced traffickers to rely more heavily on interstate highways. Local UPS and FedEx outlets, according to Lewis, have cooperated with the sheriff's office by scanning packages and allowing K-9's to sniff for drugs.

"Over the years, I have sat through hundreds of government meetings, but Mike Lewis's dramatic drug interdiction presentation highlighting the creative ways that drug smugglers conceal heroin, cocaine, and contraband has kept us talking about it to this day," said Carozza, who met the sheriff in 2003 and credits him for positioning the state at the forefront of combatting the drug trade.

The sheriff, several Maryland police chiefs, DEA (Drug Enforcement Administration) officials, and a crew from NBC News surveilled poppy fields on a visit to South America.

His commitment to border security is buoyed by concerns about Mexico's dominance of the "$420 billion drug industry worldwide," with Mexican cartels now taking over transportation of heroin, cocaine, marijuana, and methamphetamine to the US from South American countries. The cartels, for example, drove "homegrown" American meth manufacturers out of business with more potent, cheaper renditions of the drug, while deranging "THC" levels in marijuana have doubled and tripled over the years, Lewis said.

Tunnels into the southwestern United States are considered more stealth for transport than the waterways of South Florida, he explained. Lewis has trained US Border Patrol agents at numerous points of entry from Mexico, witnessing not only drug seizures but refugees stuffed in the trunks of cars. "It's possible to check only 3% of the vehicles coming across."

"Until we have border security, we will never have homeland security. We cannot allow the massive increase of illegal immigrants to continue undetected," submitted the sheriff, who has flown to the southwest with Howard Buffett, the son of billionaire Warren Buffett. Howard Buffett serves Macon County, Illinois, as a devoted law enforcement adherent and the "wealthiest" sheriff in the land.

"Things changed dramatically under the Trump administration (pertaining to the border). Obama made similar statements but never did anything to address the problem," Lewis asserted. "We are a nation of immigrants, but you can't do it in droves and grant citizenship to thirteen million illegal aliens as pledged by President Biden."

Lewis's trepidation was validated when Biden halted the construction of Trump's border wall and opened the floodgates to unescorted children, adrift people anticipating assistance from the US government, criminals, narcotics, and human-trafficking cartels.

"I knew a lot of Mexican nationals who had laughed at American stupidity," said Victor Davis Hanson, who lives in agricultural central California and wrote a positive book about Donald Trump. "They had explained to me how they crossed the border far more easily than I did when reentering the United States through customs—and with far less worry there would be consequences in lying about one's legal status." According to Hanson, $30 billion annually was being sent home by people on public support in the US.

The sheriff produced statistics from a message he delivered to the community endorsing President Trump's desire to build the wall, strongly connecting America's 300 weekly heroin deaths and 72,000 fatalities annually to opioids with drug traffickers. He cited a twoyear period when ICE (Immigration and Customs Enforcement) made 266,000 arrests of aliens with criminal records, including 100,000 assaults, 30,000 sex crimes, and 9,000 murders.

Lewis, Somerset County Sheriff Ronnie Howard, and Carozza were among the Eastern Shore officials intensely critical of lawmakers attempting to make Maryland a "sanctuary" state for undocumented immigrants in 2020.

The legislation, which Lewis described as "unconscionable," would have protected violent gangs like MS-13 that are heavily engaged in drug trafficking, from arrest, prosecution, and deportation. "Now we have MS-13, a gang who is notorious not just for killing and murdering, but they've dismantled bodies and spread these body parts all over Anne Arundel County, Prince Georges County, and Montgomery County, Maryland, in at least a dozen murders and dismemberments over the last twelve months," he said.

MS-13 (Mara Salvatrucha) was created in Los Angeles by Salvadorans who were fleeing civil war in their homeland. The gang has penetrated the United States, Canada, Central America, and Mexico.

A perennial frontrunner with Lewis at the helm, Wicomico has been only one of three Maryland counties claiming formal collaborative agreements with ICE, something the state legislature attempted to expunge in 2020.

Lewis dug in his heels: "State and local officials cooperate with federal law enforcement in every aspect such as gun control, drug laws, working closely with the FBI. Immigration should be no exception.

Shielding criminal aliens needlessly endangers innocent lives."

The sheriff and other officials are contemplating a separate location for the Wicomico County Narcotics Task Force that endeavors to eviscerate organized drug rings in the area.

A marquee moment for the task force in 2012 was the "biggest drug bust in county history," according to Lewis, culminating in an investigation that took several years. Seventy-one suspected drug dealers were indicted for state and federal offenses, prompting the sheriff to once again mention the sophisticated techniques dealers use to hide their cargo.

They were not "nickel and dime" operatives, Lewis declared. Six of the individuals warranted "kingpin" charges for being organizers, supervisors, financiers, or managers, acting as conspirators to manufacture, distribute, transport controlled substances into the state.

Cocaine, marijuana, and prescription pills with a street value of $1 million were confiscated, in addition to cash and property worth $600,000. Authorities seized firearms, ammunition, and bullet-proof armor that facilitated the nefarious transactions, he said.

"You bring drugs into Wicomico County . . . you might get away with it today; you might get away with it this week; you might get away with it next month; but I am coming for you; we are going to locate you; we are coming for you," guaranteed Lewis.

Lewis was invited to the White House seven times in eight months during Trump's tenure as a trusted law enforcement leader with widely conveyed opinions about the narcotics trade and illegal immigration. The sheriff treasured the chance to praise the president in the Oval Room for vetoing Congress's override of his national emergency declaration to stem the influx of immigrants.

"Mr. President, I can't thank you enough on behalf of America's sheriffs. This is not political propaganda. We have a dire crisis on our Southwest border, and America's sheriffs stand behind the President of the United States 100%. This is unprecedented for a president to take this kind of action."

Lewis, Chief Deputy Gary Baker, and a Worcester County judge attended the 2018 trial in New York of notorious Mexican drug lord Joaquin "El Chapo" Guzman, leader of the Sinaloa Cartel, a crime syndicate that flooded the US with contraband. Guzman was sentenced to life in prison.

The following year in Kansas City, Sheriff Lewis presented two "The FINAL Chapter for El Chapo" breakout sessions at the prestigious annual National Interdiction Conference, the largest of its kind in North America.

Lewis argues that international figures like Guzman are the source of narcotics that inevitably filter down to otherwise innocuous places like Wicomico County with a broadly dispersed population inhabiting 374 square miles.

Aaron Ross, twenty-five, of Salisbury, was sentenced to ten years in prison followed by five years of supervised release on cocaine distribution charges. Cellular phone monitoring uncovered Ross's shadowy links to New York.

Jeannine Hammett, acting agent in charge for the FBI, commended the Wicomico County Narcotics Task Force and other agencies while acknowledging the necessary fiscal tracking that occurred: "This is an important victory for the American public. The role of IRS CI (Internal Revenue Service Criminal Investigation) in narcotics investigations is to follow the money so we can financially disrupt and dismantle major drug-trafficking organizations. One of the government's most powerful weapons is the ability to seize through asset forfeiture the assets associated with narcotics-related crime. IRS Criminal Investigation is proud to provide its financial expertise as we work alongside our law enforcement partners to bring criminal justice."

Lewis recalled a spate of more than thirty vehicles that were burglarized by two juveniles and one adult in the Rustic Acres subdivision. "They (the perpetrators) said all of the cars were unlocked, so they didn't force their way into any of the vehicles. They were wearing dark clothing and had backpacks and were riding away in a cab when they got caught. They said they were looking for money to buy drugs."

An ugly microcosm of local narcotics addiction occurred when fortyeight-year-old Pittsville resident Thomas Dale Maxwell was arrested and charged for assault on a law enforcement officer, malicious destruction of property, disturbing the peace, disorderly conduct, and resisting arrest.

Reports state that Maxwell began breaking and throwing things at his residence because he ran out of medical marijuana and his parents refused to buy him more. At one point, he brandished a hatchet. Maxwell approached deputies with clenched fists, screamed profanities, and fought when they tried to restrain him. One deputy was treated for injuries at the hospital and released.

Lewis is against the decriminalization or legalization of drugs regardless of a national trend that is moving in the opposite direction. The state of Oregon, which had decriminalized marijuana years earlier, did the same for cocaine, heroin, and methamphetamine in 2020. The Western states of Oregon, California, Washington, and Colorado are already "havens" for businesses selling weed legally.

In early 2021, a bill was proposed by a Prince Georges County representative that would similarly regulate cannabis in Maryland. Jazz Lewis (no relation to Sheriff Mike Lewis) said the measure addresses social equity and racial injustices that incite the 96% arrest rate of African Americans for marijuana offenses in the state and laws "only made legal for white consumption."

Provisions of the bill also encompassed criminal justice reform, reinvestment in disadvantaged communities, and standards for "inclusion" in the recreational marijuana industry.

"Almost every heroin and cocaine addict started with misdemeanor marijuana use," Lewis maintained, regardless of race.

Sheriff Lewis and Deputy State's Attorney Bill McDermott spearheaded a local ordinance prohibiting the consumption of marijuana in vehicles and public areas, a misdemeanor charge punishable by a fine up to $500 and/or incarceration not to exceed ninety days. The goal, Lewis said, is to replicate laws pertaining to alcohol consumption even though possession of under ten grams of marijuana has been decriminalized.

"Just because marijuana now has an exception and you can possess marijuana legally by way of a medical marijuana card, it doesn't mean you should be allowed to consume marijuana in public, as the statute says, or public street fairs, sidewalks, in a shopping center or, more importantly in your vehicle," McDermott added.

Complicating America's staggering drug problem is the advent of opioid addiction in the twenty-first century. Deaths from opioid overdoses in Wicomico County have spiked by more than 33% in the last few years. According to Lewis, who created the Community Action Team (CAT) in 2015 to neutralize the odious plague, "We can't arrest ourselves out of the opioid crisis, but we won't wave the white flag. We need to chip away at it every day."

Lewis said CAT garnered an award from the Maryland Sheriffs' Association in 2016 for accruing 1,341 traffic stops and 151 criminal arrests while executing search and seizure warrants, confiscating controlled substances, and retrieving money and weapons associated with illegal narcotics transactions.

A running tally of overdoses and lives lost "year to date" is posted visibly outside the Wicomico County Sheriff's Office for motorists to see. Deputies made 550 drug-related arrests in 2019 alone, up 50% from the previous year.

In addition to the illicit opioid heroin, Wicomico County and the nation are awash with prescribed synthetic drugs like oxycodone and fentanyl whose original function was to relieve pain among cancer patients in the aftermath of surgery and trauma and during palliative care for the terminally ill instead of recreational use. OxyContin was released in the 1990s to counteract the growing black market for heroin, not unlike its predecessor methadone. Unfortunately, the "euphoric" power of opioids has hooked millions of people across the country and far too many local residents, Lewis said.

A hybrid concoction blends the resurgence of crack cocaine, a wildly popular street drug in the 1980s and 1990s, and the opioid fentanyl, which is mostly imported from China.

According to CAT officers, fifty-seven-year-old Briggett Wendell Ellis had been dealing crack as a veritable bicycle baron, delivering the drug on his two-wheeler. A search and seizure warrant on his person at Isabella and Mill streets uncovered baggies of crack, packaging material, and cash. Evidence of manufacturing the drug was found at a residence on Lake Street he frequented.

Sheriff's files show the tentacles of opioid abuse entangled a special education teacher at Parkside High School in 2017. Fiftyone-year-old Monica Snee was arrested on charges relating to heroin, oxycodone, and suboxone as she drove away from campus. Wicomico County sheriff's deputies discovered one hundred capsules, empty baggies, and $3,000 cash in the vehicle. She did not have prescriptions for the oxycodone and suboxone. Snee sold drugs throughout the county, including on school grounds, deputies said.

Lewis called Snee's behavior "an act of betrayal," saying a recovering addict and former customer of hers tipped off authorities because he wanted to stay off drugs.

Thanks to a report filed with the Child Advocacy Center in 2019, sheriff's detectives charged Elizabeth Day, a physical education instructor at James M. Bennett High School and the wife of Salisbury Mayor Jake Day, in connection with trying to purchase Adderall from a student.

Day was sentenced to ten days in jail after taking an Alford plea to attempted possession of a controlled substance. The plea meant the defendant maintained her innocence while conceding there could be sufficient evidence for conviction at a trial. The "contributing to the condition of a child" charge was dismissed.

The Wicomico County State's Attorney deferred the case to Calvert County prosecutors because the prominence of her husband created a potential conflict of interest.

Snapchat messages indicated she solicited the student for a transaction on several occasions, according to investigative records. The thirty-year-old claimed she was under emotional duress in defending her doctoral dissertation.

To an extent, Lewis correlates the opioid calamity with the perils of mental illness in Wicomico County. The Crisis Intervention Team, funded primarily by the Wicomico County Health Department, was formed to detect and evaluate health challenges that law enforcement and partner agencies encounter on a regular basis.

"Crime Intervention Team officers are trained to identify when someone may be experiencing a mental health crisis, and they'll quickly adopt strategies for these individuals," Lewis said. "This approach has been proven to dramatically decrease the risk of death to both the officers and people with mental illness, and it also reduces the number of repeated calls for service. The training demands the skills of a good social worker and an astute law enforcement officer."

President Trump declared a national health emergency in 2017 because of the opioid crisis, and two years later, the "Remove the Risk Campaign" was launched by the FDA (Food and Drug

Administration) to help Americans—especially women—to resist the temptation of abusing them at home.

In 2019, Wicomico County hosted its first annual "Goes Purple" boat parade and resource fair. Boats traveled down the Wicomico River to Brew River restaurant with vendors educating people about addiction and the fight against opioids.

At around the same time that year, three Wicomico County residents succumbed to heroin overdoses in one week, and several others were revived by naloxone. Deputies also arrested Lamont Marvin Smith and Dwight Leroy Woods on various charges after seizing 141 grams of heroin, small quantities of cocaine, and .40 caliber handgun ammunition from a home on Mount Hermon Road, Lewis said.

"I just went to a funeral this past Saturday here in Wicomico County for a little girl who died last week of a heroin overdose, something that has decimated her family. It's devasted her friends and our community," the sheriff interjected. "There are many people that are crying out for help. A lot of depressed individuals out there. Losing their jobs, losing their businesses, and in many cases, losing their homes."

But Lewis conveyed frustration over addicts wallowing in their circumstances: "There are just as many people who don't want our help. They don't want our intervention. They enjoy being a heroin addict. They enjoy being on the cusp of death."

Achieving the "buy-in" of doctors and pharmacists to closely monitor excessive consumption of prescribed opioids is a work in progress. Ever vigilant, Sheriff Lewis has pushed Wicomico County officials to join a national lawsuit against major pharmaceutical companies that profit handsomely from the distribution and sale of opioids.

Mirroring comments about the eradication of destructive drugs, Lewis shared a voice message from a police officer in rural New York state, complimenting the sheriff for training that enabled him to perform a large drug seizure during a traffic stop and asking for additional advice concerning narcotics enforcement. "I'll be calling him back when our interview is finished," Lewis said pridefully about the acumen that ascended his career.

CHAPTER TWO

SHOWCASING THE WICOMICO COUNTY
SHERIFF'S OFFICE

Lewis praised Sheriff Nelms for serving the county faithfully and effectively. He was interested, however, in transitioning the Wicomico County Sheriff's Office from primarily serving warrants and furnishing court bailiffs to a full-service agency. "As sheriff, you can change so much," he said. "The buck stops with me. I have a front-row seat to the greatest show on earth."

Maciarello said Lewis was instrumental in transforming Salisbury from one of the five most dangerous communities in America per capita (according to *Neighborhood Scout*) into a community that barely makes the worst one hundred. "His leadership, experience, and sheer gravitas enhanced teamwork that was required."

Crime patterns, with implications for the strategic deployment of Wicomico County sheriff's deputies, are charted and analyzed at the sheriff's office in seven patrol sectors, traditionally known as "zones" in law enforcement vernacular:

1. Salisbury, Allen, Dear Harbor, Fruitland, Fox Chase;
2. Parsonsburg, Delmar;
3. Delmar, Log Cabin, Adkins Road;

4. Nanticoke, Waterview, White Haven, Tyaskin;

5. Booth Street, Reservation;

6. Hebron, Mardela Springs, Sharptown; and

7. Pittsville, Willards, Powellville

The number of monthly calls for service in the respective sectors is available on the agency's website.

Pivotal to solving crimes is the Criminal Investigation Division (CID) which, beyond normal investigative methods includes "interviews and interrogation; use of arrest and search warrants; [a] database for pertinent information, evidence seizure and collection, and use of informants. Detectives also utilize the Maryland State Police Forensic Division and Crime Scene Technicians for the collection, processing, and analysis of evidence."

The mission statement of Lewis and the sheriff's office clarifies the aspiration "to remain focused on our core purpose to preserve peace, seek justice, and improve quality of life for all by providing exceptional law enforcement service."

According to the National Sheriffs' Association, in 1652, Northampton, Virginia, on the Eastern Shore became the first American county to elect a sheriff. With the exception of a few town marshals, the sheriff is the only law enforcement executive directly accountable to the voting populace. Among other principles, the organization affirms that sheriffs must not abdicate "responsibilities, duties, or management rights to other governmental entities, unions or political influence."

The first Wicomico County sheriff was William Howard, a Quantico farmer. The term limit for sheriff was originally two years, although statutes allowed multiple terms non-consecutively. The duration jumped to four years in 1926 when the prohibition against sequenced terms was deleted. The early sheriffs received free housing in the county courthouse but were unpaid. Actual crime-fighting was left primarily to the Salisbury Police Department.

Like many places in America, the role of sheriff's offices changed gradually with population growth in outlying areas. Jesse Pollitt was considered the first "modern" sheriff in the 1940s and 1950s, bolstering public confidence with marked patrol units and a higher arrest rate. Sheriff Graham was elected in 1958, expanding the number of deputies from four to eight and starting night patrol, as the relatively remote Delmarva Peninsula witnessed an insidious influx of narcotics and criminals from Baltimore, Washington, D.C., and Philadelphia.

The notorious killer of Sheriff Graham, however, lived in Hebron and had been arrested for stealing a television from a downtown Salisbury store. With the weapon supplied covertly by his girlfriend, twenty-one-year-old James Bartholomey fatally shot Deputy Albert Kelly through the bars of his jail cell during a security check and gunned down Sheriff Graham who had bolted out of his office to find out what was going on. The inmate fled down the back stairs of the courthouse where the jail was located and then sprinted up a deserted Salisbury street on an otherwise quiet Sunday evening.

Authorities launched a manhunt, said to be of unprecedented proportions for the Eastern Shore. Delaware State Police tracked the suspect to a Dover motel where he was holed up, storming his room and recovering the .22 pistol used in the homicides.

According to the sheriff's office, Bartholomey was sentenced to die in the gas chamber but ended up in prison because the state of Maryland suspended the death penalty. His girlfriend, Connie Beckner, nineteen, and Davis Hudson, who helped the killer escape in a car, both did time for being accessories to the carnage. In a bizarre twist of irony, only hours before the murders, the Salisbury *Daily Times* had published a prominent article saying the county jail was outdated and susceptible to safety breaches, a notion that Sheriff Graham denied.

In addition to their legacy in Wicomico County, Sheriff Sam Graham and Deputy Albert Kelly are honored by law enforcement endeavors such as "Officer Down Memorial Page" and "Never Forgotten" for their sacrifice.

Sheriff Lewis displays a picture of his father, the other deputies on the force, and Sheriff Graham in his office.

Although the jail is operated separately now by a warden as the Wicomico County Detention Center, upgrading the sheriff's office and establishing a distinctive, polished, and forward-thinking "brand" has been essential to forging a credible twenty-first-century law enforcement agency, Lewis said.

The new dark gray uniforms are stalwart and stylish. In fact, the sheriff's office received a "best dressed" award among 235 entries in various categories from the North American Association of Uniform Manufacturers and Distributors. Contrary to prevailing political correctness, Lewis restored the Wicomico 'Indian" insignia on the shirt sleeves and sheriff's star, arguing it celebrates the heritage of the area rather than impugning a race of people.

The antiquated, decrepit fleet of old white patrol cars was overhauled for sexier black-and-white Dodge Chargers today costing nearly $60,000 with data terminals, computers, cameras, Tasers, flashlights, chopsticks for obstructing fleeing vehicles, sophisticated radar, and weapons storage. They are high performance, accelerating from a virtual standstill to 140 miles an hour if necessary. All sheriff's vehicles are pragmatically adorned in vinyl to safely remove vomit, blood, urine, and other health hazards. Most recently, emergency lights have been installed in the interior of sheriff's vehicles, replacing more cumbersome and vulnerable ones attached on the outside. Some of the SUVs display barely discernible sheriff's office logos called "ghost graphics" that lights up fluorescently in the evening. These are referred to as "subdued vehicles" by local officers.

The "ghost" option is a hybrid, of sorts, straddling the line between marked and unmarked units. Completely marked units, Lewis explained, present a visual crime deterrent while reassuring residents that their neighborhoods are being patrolled by the sheriff's office. Unmarked vehicles enable more stealth operatives such as SWAT and tactical squads. "People are also less fearful to talk to our deputies in the unmarked units, knowing it isn't quite as obvious to other residents what they are doing."

Indeed, the professionalism of the Wicomico County Sheriff's Office has instilled confidence in the people it serves.

"He (the sheriff) strikes me as a strong figure which is what the position and the community need," Norma Dobrowlowski said. "The sheriff and his deputies have made a point to be familiar with our neighborhood and any issues we have had."

"He and his deputies are well-respected. When duty calls, he is a fierce defender of the law. His constituents know he would lay down his life to save someone," Pollitt said.

Lewis, upon recently hearing from an elderly woman who wasn't totally satisfied with the response to her call about a possible prowler, personally conducted a security check of the home and property. The resident thanked him in a handwritten note.

Not surprisingly in his line of work, congeniality and kudos sometimes evade the equation. He was eating at a restaurant in street clothes with his father when their server kept staring sternly at the sheriff. "He finally asked if I was Mike Lewis, and I said yes. Then, he told me I had arrested him on the bypass years ago. It was very stressful for my dad, and he got a permit to carry."

Understandably, Lewis and his family sometimes socialize away from Wicomico County to achieve privacy. And when he anticipates situations that could invoke hostility, Lewis is occasionally accompanied by one of three robust deputies. Rest assured, the energized, high-profile sheriff is always armed.

For the most part, the fifty-six-year-old has allayed rumors that he might seek higher office. "It is always a possibility," he said cautiously. "What I can say is that my family has given me unconditional support all of my years in the profession and that my wife's feelings are first and foremost."

The sheriff flirted momentarily with the notion of running for governor or the U.S. Congress, but his wife of thirty-four years,

Denise, said she had no desire to live in Washington, D.C., let alone listen to her husband advance political views vociferously on national television.

"I love being sheriff. I ran for sheriff out of genuine concern for the county and am humbled to know the people have put their trust in me," Lewis said effusively.

His quest to gain trust was displayed when a black sixteen-yearold resident collapsed and died behind Fulton Hall on the Salisbury University campus. The teenager was being pursued by college students who believed he had stolen a bike from the University Park housing complex. Social media erupted in the supposition that the students had beaten him to death. Lewis personally met with a large group of emotionally distraught family members and friends to explain there was no sign of trauma, that one of the students attempted to revive the teenager, and the autopsy determined the cause of death had been cardiac arrest.

Lewis's Wicomico County friends and sources are known to contact him directly with information about crimes. As the page turned mercifully to the 2021 New Year, a suspicious "targeted act of violence" death was reported in the enclave of Hebron. Lewis said, "I received a phone call from a female subject who wished to only speak to me regarding specific details she had about the case. We are working very aggressively on the case. We are tracking down all leads, and we are confident we will solve the case."

He "mentored" an eleven-year-old boy who witnessed the fatal shooting of his mother by her ex-boyfriend. Deputies arrested the killer, and he was sentenced to life in prison. On the way to the funeral, according to the sheriff, "(Malik) wanted to use my police radio. I let him, not knowing what he wanted to say. So he gets on the radio and says, 'I just want to thank all the cops who came to my house and saved my life. I want to thank you all for getting the guy who killed my mother.'"

"Sheriff Mike Lewis ranks as one of the most popular elected officials in Wicomico County history. His popularity is such that he has run for re-election three times without opposition," wrote Greg Bassett, editor and general manager of the *Salisbury Independent* weekly newspaper. "Personal, engaging, and charismatic, he is one of those rare people difficult to overlook. The sheriff excels at making his presence known, and when he begins to speak, it's impossible to close your ears."

"Sheriff Lewis's connection and ties to the community were invaluable when I served as State's Attorney," Maciarello said. "He never seemed to say no to anyone if they asked him to come to their event or to speak. He would say, 'Well Matthew, first I am going to the Elks for an Eagle Scout Ceremony; then, I'm off to the Lions for their muskrat dinner; then, I'm going to this church for their annual bazaar, then off to greet the Wounded Warriors who are riding into town.'"

Councilman Cannon referred to Lewis as "dynamically proactive," balancing crime-fighting obligations with "endless appearances at local events, media releases, and public appearances with the local governing body."

The sheriff cherishes special events like "Remembering Our Fallen Heroes" on Memorial Day, which attracts hundreds of people, and waving happily to the Christmas parade crowd despite a handful of protesters haranguing the police.

The versatile sheriff moderated a town hall hosted by Congressman Andy Harris at Wicomico High School in 2017. Months earlier, the Maryland Republican legislator's appearance at Chesapeake College in Wye Mills was acrimonious. Lewis was compelled to intercede on only a couple of occasions in Salisbury. He allowed a cadre of Harris's opposition to gather at tables outside the premises; no disturbance occurred, and access remained unfettered. Lewis said many of the same people had vilified him weeks prior for "divisive rhetoric."

Lewis has lobbied effectively for a new $30.7 million sheriff's office on ten acres with superior access to the US 50 bypass and the business US 50 route through the middle of Salisbury. "The present facility (on Naylor Mill Road) is failing," he said. "We're in an old steel building. The ceiling continues to leak. We just spent thousands of dollars to have the roof water-proofed and it's still leaking. We're covering things up in plastic, even my office, and setting trashcans up when it rains heavily. You can't operate like that. We have outgrown this building."

The criminal investigation unit is rapidly expanding in uncomfortably limited confines, according to Lewis, with conversations and important interrogations lacking sufficient confidentiality. Holding areas aren't even spacious enough to separate juvenile and adult suspects.

Square footage will nearly triple, from 13,000 to 38,000, with construction slated for completion in 2022. Budgetary constraints, due partially to the pandemic, have delayed the project for more than a year.

The designated location, selected over property behind the Shorebirds Stadium several miles to the east, is also in close proximity to highcrime areas on the west side of Salisbury. "We receive the bulk of our calls in the African American community," Lewis said.

Fourteen-year deputy Benjamin Jones was absolved of culpability in the fatal shooting of a suspect on the west end. Jones responded to a report of a woman being threatened by a gun-wielding man on Olivia Street. Fednel Rhinvil ran away when Jones approached him for questioning. The deputy gave chase, and a physical altercation ensued as Rhinvil attempted to scale a fence. Rhivil drew a handgun during the scuffle and Jones shot him. The deputy sustained a broken finger.

"This office deems the officer's version of events to be very credible," State's Attorney Maciarello reported. "It is quite clear that any reasonable officer in Jones' position would have perceived that Rhinvil was about to use his loaded and operational .22 caliber revolver. Rhivil's use of this weapon presented an imminent and deadly threat."

Sheriff Lewis was characteristically blunt in his assessment: "Fednel Rhinvil was a clear threat to the community, especially those residents on the west side of Salisbury and those sworn to protect them. I thank God that our deputy was not more seriously injured. We will no longer be threatened by the menace known as Fednel Rhinvil."

"It is very important to note that he (the sheriff) was always tremendously respectful of the office of state's attorney. We agreed on many things, and on some things we certainly challenged each other," Maciarello said. "Steel sharpens steel, and one makes another better, wiser."

A candlelight vigil was held in the same neighborhood for Stephon Hagans, thirty-one, found shot to death in front of his home on Dale Lane. The murder, which occurred just before Christmas in 2019, remains unsolved.

The early morning gunfire was heard by residents, and there were reports of the assailants fleeing the area in a white vehicle.

"I'm asking people to please assist us and bring closure to Stefon's family," a compassionate Lewis said. "They deserve that, and there's someone out there who certainly knows what happened. We do not believe there is a larger threat to the community."

In October 2020, the body of Trisha Lyn Parker, the mother of ten children, was seen by a neighbor floating in Johnson Pond on the west side. A boyfriend, twenty-three-year-old Marquez Labronte Armstrong, told Wicomico County sheriff's detectives he had choked and punched her to death.

"They had been arguing over money," Lewis explained. "It was challenging because of all the crime scenes we had to process."

Following the fatal attack that occurred at the woman's home, investigative reports show, Armstrong tossed her clothes in a dumpster. With the help of alleged accomplice Corey Lamar Jones, eighteen, her body was transported in a van to the pond and thrown in the water. The suspects used an accelerant to burn the van and hide evidence. Jones also assisted in cleaning up the scene of the beating, even stealing her television and a computer.

Murder, assault, disposal of a human body, arson, and malicious burning charges were filed against both suspects.

While enhancing the response time for deputies to high-crime neighborhoods is crucial to the new site, the Child Advocacy Center in downtown Salisbury, the fugitive warrants division operated concurrently with the US Marshals Service, and other emerging response and provider entities also bespeak the need for superior accommodations.

The risks of serving on the US Marshals Service Capital Area Regional Fugitive Task Force were evident when Wicomico Sheriff's Deputy Thomas Funk attempted to arrest a Maryland man wanted for multiple felonies, Lewis said. Tavone Dobson wounded Funk in the arm after a woman allowed the officer to enter a residence in Cambridge, twenty miles north of Wicomico County. Funk returned fire without hitting the suspect, broke out a window, leaped onto the roof, and jumped to safety. Reports show he had pulled a mattress and dresser between himself and the assailant while trying to keep an innocent victim on the floor from being shot. Dobson fired numerous times from inside the house at task force members outside, finally surrendering several hours later.

Lewis was upset that the US Marshals didn't inform him immediately about the shooting of a deputy. "I heard about it from chatter on the police radio. They should have called me directly. Dobson was wanted in two states, including murder with a firearm in Cambridge."

The National Sheriffs' Association awarded Deputy Funk the Medal of Valor and Purple Heart for his bravery.

The sheriff's forays and Funk's testimonial to the county council insisted upon disability coverage for deputies injured or incapacitated on the job.

"I faced a man who shot and attempted to kill me," implored Funk. "My biggest fear after being shot, bleeding in the back of an ambulance, was losing my home where I live with my wife and daughter."

Wicomico County Executive Bob Culver's subsequent announcement was endearing to deputies: "The Wicomico County Sheriff's Office, under the leadership of Sheriff Mike Lewis, continues to do an outstanding job protecting our community with a professional force of men and women. We have just completed a five-year collective bargaining agreement with the Fraternal Order of Police that will provide disability benefits for deputies as well as competitive salaries that will help ensure our best law enforcement officers will stay in our county to protect and to serve."

"Operation: On the Lam(b)" and "Operation: Hide and Seek," chiefly funded by the Governor's Office of Crime Control and Prevention, netted 107 arrests of fugitives in Wicomico and Dorchester counties by the Maryland State Police, the sheriff's office, and assorted law enforcement agencies in 2019.

For motorists who feel inconvenienced and annoyed by traffic stops, Lewis contends they are invaluable to law enforcement searching for fugitives and felons and not made indiscriminately. Despite their ultimate desire to intercept and incarcerate hardened criminals, deputies cannot ignore violations by otherwise law-abiding citizens.

"Do not get confrontational out on the roadway. It does not satisfy your goals or our goals, and you're going to end up being arrested," Lewis advised. "It is best to stay in your car when you are stopped. We want to go home safely to our families at night, and we want you to do the same."

Too many law enforcement officers are injured, maimed, or killed each year in America making traffic stops that turn up narcotics, dead bodies, and stolen property, among other incriminating things, Lewis said. "It is nerve-wracking not always knowing who or what we are dealing with—the scariest thing we do. We don't know what kind of day the person is having [or] what might be going on in their life."

Lewis said he reminds students in his training seminars, such as the one held at the Alabama Sheriffs' Association annual convention, that "Four out of five serious crimes in the United States involve transportation." Primary categories of the sheriff's instruction are observing a violation, criminality profiling versus racial profiling, tending to enforcement action, searching the vehicle, officer safety, and preparing for prosecution.

"Sheriff Lewis was great. Our guys that work the street that are in this class . . . they are exchanging information, and it is great to see," said Lieutenant Brendan Hall of the Berkeley County, West Virginia, Sheriff's Department following an expert presentation on traffic stops and drug interdiction. Hall said municipal police officers, deputies, and troopers from Maryland and West Virginia participating in the session were impressed knowing that Lewis was essential as a trooper to a federal case that indicted forty-four people for trafficking nearly ten tons of cocaine across the US.

"I think Berkeley County, West Virginia, and the Washington County area of Hagerstown in Maryland—and this whole region—is a very target-enriched environment for drug traffickers," Lewis detailed. "We have an interstate system that allows these drug traffickers to travel every day, to and from populated cities, into our small communities, to poison our children. We can do a better job at what we do."

Among other recent regional assignments, Sheriff Lewis has trained officers from fourteen agencies in Fulton County, New York, and spoken to the New York State Stop DWI Foundation. Nearly two hundred law enforcement personnel attended his traffic control presentation in Wilson, North Carolina.

A staple of Lewis's seminars is the recommendation that officers approach the passenger side of the vehicle for better, broader surveillance rather than the riskier "fatal funnel" on the driver's side. "Keep your hands visible, and turn on your interior lights at night to make it safer for everyone."

"I can be talked into a ticket and I can be talked out of a ticket," Lewis added as he recounted a recent speeding motorist on the bypass from Crisfield, Maryland, who only received a warning from him because of politeness and civility.

"People are always putting it on law enforcement. The public needs to learn. Your attitude is everything," emphasized the sheriff.

Lewis is a certified master instructor on traffic stops with the National Highway Traffic Safety Administration and has been officially recognized in that realm by state and federal courts.

The sheriff's office completed 710 "special enforcement" traffic assignments requested by the citizens of Wicomico County in 2020.

"Now as a State Senator, I continue to benefit from Sheriff Lewis's counsel and example of perseverance," Carozza said while referencing Wade's Law, which she has proposed to criminalize negligent driving for the sake of protecting victims and their families.

It isn't unusual for deputies to nab repeat DUI offenders during traffic stops. Kevin Murray, Michelle Mezick, and Stevie Jackson were arrested within twenty-four hours of one another on Wicomico County roadways, sheriff's office records show.

Murray's vehicle was straddling the southbound lanes of South Salisbury Boulevard. He refused a breathalyzer, and his car didn't have an ignition interlock device required of convicted drunk drivers. Mezick, who had three prior alcohol-related driving convictions, ran a stop sign on Glen Avenue, drove over a grassy area, and into a parking lot before her arrest. Jackson attempted to elude a deputy, tossed a cup out the window, ran two stop signs, spun out, and finally stopped at West Road and Naylor Mill Road, not far from the Wicomico County Sheriff's Office. An open container of alcohol was in the vehicle, and he blew a .15 on the breathalyzer. Jackson had been convicted twice of drinking and driving in the past.

The perils of drinking and driving were arguably more acute when Michael Walker, twenty-six, was also arrested for DUI on Naylor Mill Road. Deputies clocked Walker at seventy-four miles per hour in a forty-maximum speed limit zone with a two-year-old child inside the car.

A car reportedly plowed into the back of a sheriff's SUV at the intersection of South Division Street and Dykes Road early on Valentine's Day of 2021. Michael John Belich, twenty-nine, of Salisbury, was charged with DWI, impairment, negligence, and failure to curtail his speed. Belich, whose blood alcohol level was nearly three times the legal limit, said he was just trying to get home.

The deputy was treated for minor injuries at the hospital and released. Both vehicles were towed from the scene.

With the Chesapeake Bay Bridge as a backdrop on Kent Island, Sheriff Lewis delivered an impassioned, typically eloquent statement about motorists who "check-in their common sense at the Bay Bridge" before visiting the Eastern Shore in the summer. He championed a collective effort among sheriff's deputies, state police, and state transportation officers in the "Bay to Beach" campaign to eliminate not only drunk drivers but those who text and talk on their cell phones while operating motor vehicles. The message and power of his personality captivated local residents using social media:

> "What a class act."
>
> "This is the man. Listen to that message."
>
> "Great message, Sheriff Lewis!"
>
> "I think he would be great as a leader at either state or national level. But I think being a law enforcement or security position of some sort is where he excels."
>
> "Marylanders need a man like Sheriff Lewis to be our next governor. I'm willing to bet he'd make the streets of Baltimore safe again."
>
> "He's a bad dude. Best we've ever had."
>
> *www.facebook.com/wicomicosheriff*

Lewis's flair contributes to avid media interest in the Wicomico County Sheriff's Office. "I respect the media. I need the media, and the media needs me. Most of our local media and reporters are not trying to burn us. We maintain a positive relationship."

Salisbury *Daily Times* reporter Ricky Pollitt agreed: "Sheriff Lewis has always been very open and responsive to media inquiries. He is prompt and vigilant when it comes to informing the media of pressing matters. He understands the media is the bridge between his office and the public."

The sheriff's willingness to receptively engage local media was illustrated when he educated veteran television journalist Jimmy Hoppa about the vagaries of traffic stops.

Lewis said he briefed *Daily Times* reporter Vanessa Junkin on the tricks of concealment after personally detaining a minivan because it was following a box truck too closely on US 13 near Zion Road. Sheriff's records revealed that both occupants of the vehicle had extensive criminal histories for distribution of narcotics, and $46,000 cash was discovered.

The sheriff has told his command staff from the beginning that punctually, transparently providing facts to the media is better than having them derive potentially erroneous information from other sources. The "Community Press" moniker invoked by the sheriff's office implies an inclusive approach toward citizens and the media.

"We must be forthright," he stressed.

Lieutenant Robinson is the agency's main media conduit, interfacing with newspaper, television, and radio outlets, logging timely updates on social media platforms such as Facebook and Twitter, and monitoring the sheriff's office website, which was designed by students at Salisbury Christian School. Lewis commended Robinson, who doubles as patrol commander, for cordially and deftly handling media inquiries.

Robinson said he and the sheriff are usually "on the same page" concerning media releases. "We like to show the good work that the sheriff's office is doing every day. And we let people know when our deputies are assaulted, cussed, and called racially disparaging names."

Novel stories sometimes garner the greatest media feedback according to Robinson, the agency's equivalent of a uniformed, sworn Public Information Officer (PIO). A Washington, D.C., television reporter complimented a release he drafted that said rowdies outside the courthouse were "gesticulating" a "half peace" sign rather than giving law enforcement "the finger" as they jumped on the hoods of patrol cars.

A citizen told a deputy to "go fuck" himself, something Robinson politely and humorously pointed out to another news outfit was "physically impossible" to do.

Trending national stories occasionally bring attention to Wicomico County. CNN contacted Robinson about a press release mentioning fisticuffs over girls' softball as "adults" around the nation were embarrassing themselves living vicariously through the sports forays of their children. A New Jersey man, whose daughter had been kicked off the team in part because of his misconduct, confronted the father of the girl's former teammate who was competing at a tournament in Salisbury. The aggressor in the fracas was dropped like a shirt off a hanger by his rival.

"Some believe Sheriff Lewis seeks the spotlight, appearing on American commentator Sean Hannity's show in the past," Pollitt said.

"However, by looking at what he and his department have done since 2006, it couldn't be more the opposite. He is a watchful protector, a strong representative of law enforcement, and a friend to all."

The spotlight shone brightly and creatively on retiring Deputy Dave Goldberg in a recorded video clip. Goldberg received a congratulatory call from dispatch as he was sitting in his patrol car, exchanging authentic police 10-code and thanking his colleagues. "At 12:01 hours today's date, you are officially 10-42," stated the dispatcher, meaning his "shift" with the Wicomico County Sheriff's Office was truly over.

Heightening public enthusiasm for the sheriff and his deputies while safeguarding the community is the *Crime Stoppers* program on Pac 14 community access television, featuring profiles provided by the Salisbury and Fruitland police departments and sheriff's office of wanted fugitives with mugshots, physical descriptions, outstanding charges, and latest verified location. People furnishing information about the suspects may remain anonymous when they call the twentyhour "tip line."

At one juncture, deputies arrested four at-large suspects in three days. "Normally, we may get one a week. To get this many apprehensions is phenomenal. It says something about the community—that they are working with us," said Lieutenant Robinson, beaming. "For some of them, we don't have good addresses. Some are deceptive addresses, or they move and don't leave a forwarding address. We are very pleased the public sees these photos about these cases and are willing to call in tips to help us find them."

Many vital concerns are now pursued by the public through the Wicomico County Sheriff's Office app available as a free download from iPhone and Android stores, encouraging citizens to receive instantaneous alerts, news, and public safety resources. Lewis thanked the Wicomico County Local Management Board for funding the initiative.

The "submit a tip" option also allows people to anonymously volunteer information about Wicomico County's Most Wanted Fugitives. There is a map pinpointing known sex offenders, status updates regarding inmates, and victim notifications. COVID-19 information, accident reports, social media feeds, and the locations of law enforcement and fire agencies are also displayed.

"In today's technologically-oriented world, mobile apps are the most important and innovative way to communicate," Lewis said. "We have created the Wicomico County Sheriff's Office mobile app to keep our community informed and alerted to emergency situations, and to engage our citizens to be our partners in public safety." Regarding transparency, Lewis was undaunted when he learned the ACLU (American Civil Liberties Union) had released several versions of an app that automatically transmit audio and video interaction between law enforcement officers and civilians to servers. "Anything I can do to better professionalize the Wicomico County Sheriff's Office and our profession, I'm all for it. I don't want rogue deputies working for me."

"Home" at the Wicomico County Sheriff's Office Facebook page not only provides ongoing public service announcements, information about wanted felons, missing persons, arrests, and other law enforcement matters; it stimulates dialogue with appreciative residents:

> "Strong work! Keep our communities safe!"
>
> "Not a good idea to commit a crime in this county. Not much slips by. Take that violence somewhere else. Thanks."
>
> "Do the crime, do the time. Plain and simple."
>
> "Making officers put themselves in danger against trash like this and he'll end up getting six months probation an doing it again. He can't earn $100–$500 legitimately."
>
> "Great job sheriff's office for getting them off the streets."
>
> "Police lock these guys up and the courts dump them right back in our laps."
>
> "I stand behind the Blue! Thank you for all you do and the ones at home waiting for you to come home safe!" "Wicomico County Deputies are the best"
>
> *www.facebook.com/wicomicosheriff*

A Facebook booking photo showed two gashes and significant swelling on the face of a forty-four-year-old white Mardela man who punched a deputy several times. Responding deputies observed that a female had been assaulted by the suspect. He then violently resisted arrest and continued to make threats after being handcuffed. Multiple assault charges were filed, and bond was set at $20,000.

> The report elicited plenty of comments:
>
> "Looks like he got lucky, only one side of his face got it. Glad the deputies weren't hurt worse and I hope the victim is ok and doesn't go back unless it's to beat him while he sleeps. With a bat!"

"Should have been no bond."

"If you resist you get what you get—white, black, purple, or blue."

"I see the Jim Beam gave him a little too much courage." "Well done deputies! Well done Sheriff's office!"

www.facebook.com/wicomicosheriff

The agency's Facebook page encouraged locals to "be the driver that saves lives" by "handing off" the car keys to someone sober when imbibing during the 2021 Super Bowl.

The importance of piquing citizen awareness through social media was amplified in 2020 during a phone scam. The chicanery involved imposters using the names of actual Wicomico sheriff's deputies telling recipients of the calls that they were subject to arrest warrants issued by the circuit court unless fines were paid instantly. The scammers even created a caller ID to mimic local phone numbers. The sheriff's office reminded residents that it would never make such demands.

While fervently advancing programs for engaging the public in a non-enforcement capacity, Lewis defends the "militarization" of today's law enforcement, saying police are often "outgunned" by citizens brandishing high-powered weapons on the streets, in their automobiles, and homes. "Along with building a sense of professionalism and safety that we are able to protect the public, people also need to know that when we tell you that you are under arrest, we need to take you into custody whether it is voluntary or you resist."

The sheriff reminds naysayers that law enforcement agencies are "quasi-military" in terms of bearing, discipline, rank, and command structure. There is a reason, he said, that a significant number of deputies and officers are veterans of the military.

The agency mourned the "sudden and untimely" death of former Marine Steven Ray, forty-two, only twenty-four hours after his last assignment as a deputy with the Wicomico County Sheriff's Office. Ray left behind three sons, a girlfriend of many years, and four siblings.

"As sheriff of Wicomico County, I ask that you keep Deputy Ray in your thoughts and prayers, as they will be experiencing many difficult days ahead. Thank you, Stevie Ray, for serving the citizens of Wicomico County with distinction and pride. Semper Fi," Lewis wrote.

A crowning achievement for Sheriff Lewis was securing the "long overdue" MRAP (Mine Resistant-Ambush Protected) combat support vehicle from the federal government's 10-33 program that donates military equipment to law enforcement. The MRAP, which originally cost $1.2 million and should have been $450,000 in used condition, was obtained by the Wicomico County Sheriff's Office for free. "We did spend $6,000 hauling it here on a flatbed from Fort Hood in Texas," he said.

"Despite pleas to our congressmen to fund an armored vehicle that I could make available to the entire Delmarva Peninsula, it fell on deaf ears until 10-33 came along."

He heralded its utility in responding to mass shootings in malls, churches, schools, and other venues where people congregate in large numbers.

Lewis posed a question to skeptics: "Walking into protests and situations that are increasingly violent, why shouldn't we be able to have vehicles to extricate cops and citizens to safety?"

While recounting the vitriol directed at Lewis for procuring the MRAP, the necessity for one was evident when a gunman rained down bullets on his own family and law enforcement officers before a comparable military vehicle arrived belatedly from Dover Air Force Base, Maciarello said.

The MRAP was housed initially at the Maryland State Police barracks in Salisbury, and is now protected and shielded from public view on the grounds of the Wicomico County Sheriff's Office.

Never receding from improvisation, the sheriff's office also converted the Wicomico County Bookmobile into a mobile command center.

In addition, the agency has obtained shotguns, rifles, and M-16's at Sheriff Lewis's behest.

Lewis is a huge proponent of K-9 police dogs. "Dogs have 900% greater sensitivity in their noses than humans. They can detect a teaspoon of sugar in one million gallons of water, which is two Olympic-size swimming pools. Instead of an aggregate smell of a pot of soup, for instance, a dog can decipher each of the ingredients separately," he said.

Lewis enjoyed being a guest speaker at a graduation for New Jersey K-9 officers, reminding them to ensure the constitutional rights of suspects.

Since taking over as sheriff, Lewis said, the agency has "raised the bar" on traffic stops utilizing K-9's. Most importantly, "If a K-9 detects the presence of drugs, you have probable cause to search without a warrant. This has led to huge seizures of cash and drugs."

Sheriff's K-9 units have assisted other departments in numerous investigations. He called dogs "game changers" regarding perception and enforcement. "Drug dealers know what they are capable of, and things are less likely to escalate when (the dogs) are present. They are trained to protect an officer who is being assaulted."

One of the dogs specializes in bomb detection, four focus primarily on drugs, and three are cross-trained to detect guns, Lewis said.

"Elon" was a celebrated K-9 who retired in 2014 after contributing to three hundred arrests and seizures of money and contraband totaling $48,000.

"Uke" followed suit at the age of nine, a sad moment for handler and K-9 deputy Jeff Heath, with whom he lived. "I am blessed that Uke always had a watchful eye on me," Heath said. "I never deployed him, but we had numerous surrenders when some gave up so they don't get bitten. He's only sixty-five pounds, but he could take down someone well over three hundred pounds."

The family of Deputy John Brune started the annual K-9 foundation fundraiser in his honor. One of the sheriff's office's dogs was named Brune for the victim of a heart attack at his home in the rural enclave of Willards.

In January 2021, the sheriff's office mourned the death of Flasko, who faithfully served Deputy Matt Jones, the agency, and the community by conducting nearly one thousand "scans" for the presence of illegal drugs over eight years.

Jones and Deputy Shelly Lewis were recently promoted to the rank of corporal, with Corporal Jordan Banks becoming a newly-minted sergeant.

Lewis commended Deputy J.C. Richardson for being an esteemed K-9 trainer serving the Wicomico County Sheriff's Office and the Mid-Atlantic region.

Not all dogs in Wicomico County have been deployed in an official capacity. The frailties of the human condition never cease to amaze law enforcement, including the sheriff's office when it investigated the "puppy mill" in unincorporated Eden.

Seventy-year-old Susan Murphy pleaded guilty in 2019 to twenty-six charges of animal cruelty. Three hundred dogs, mostly Pomeranians, were found at her home lacking adequate care, their fur matted with feces amid piles of excrement. She was sentenced to sixty days in jail, ten months of home detention, and three years suspended probation, mandating forfeiture of all animals on the property other than chickens, parrots, and two aging cats.

Authorities transported the dogs from the premises to the Wicomico County Humane Society, where mounds of toys, treats, and detergent were kindly donated by residents.

Lieutenant Robinson adopted one of the Pomeranians, naming him Roger and marveling at his "remarkable" transformation. A Facebook group was formed for people who liberated the dogs from their misery by providing them new homes.

Roger's death in January 2021 was heartbreaking for Robinson's entire family. They tried everything to reverse his health. "The sheriff called us that evening to see how we were doing," said the emotional

Robinson.

From canines to equines, the Wicomico County Sheriff's Office has been at the pinnacle of investigations involving animal abuse.

Conceivably more egregious than the Murphy case was what transpired on the two-acre farm outside Quantico owned by seventyfive-year-old Barbara Pilchard. Sheriff Lewis and an official from the Wicomico County Humane Society were dispatched after a neighbor complained about the condition of horses on the property.

Lewis reported observing twenty-five dead, decomposing horses and probably another hundred roaming around. "Those horses were so hungry, they had broken sliding doors in the back of the house trying to get in and find something to eat," Lewis said—and others tried to eat the aluminum siding of a building.

Surviving mares and foals were taken to a safer, albeit undisclosed location while the grim task of removing the dead bodies was consummated.

He said the expanse of the devastation was revealed by a videographer shooting footage in the WBOC-TV helicopter circling above the site.

In the past, Pilchard's horses were known to escape their pasture and graze in people's gardens. Two hundred forlorn, starving cats had also been rescued from the residence.

Pilchard was fined $13,000 and placed on five years of supervised probation for committing animal cruelty, neglect/insufficient food, and neglect/insufficient veterinary care.

Lewis agreed with area residents who considered the punishment too light. He convinced the county council to unanimously pass a new ordinance strengthening the ability of law enforcement to access and scrutinize conditions on suspect properties. State laws are relatively flexible, providing owners significant discretion in taking care of their horses.

The sheriff promised vigilance: "I take this personally. Our command staff is on top of any report of animal abuse. We were so distraught about what happened. We'll never allow this to happen again on my watch."

County Executive Culver personally visited the Pilchard farm, describing the gruesome fate of a foal that died near the front door of the house: "That foal was still-born. And the mother, she threw her head up and just wailed. I looked at her, and I could see the hurt in her eyes. She kept nudging the foal, trying to help get it up. But it was dead. It was so sad, and there was nothing we could do."

Lewis said there was no more outstanding law enforcement advocate than Culver, who died recently of liver cancer at sixty-seven. "He wept in my office [as we discussed the illness]," bemoaned Lewis, having tactfully inquired about Culver's dramatic weight loss in the past. "He said he had six months to live. We knew we were losing a law enforcement ally."

Lewis recounted his comments as informal master of ceremonies at the wake: "Bob knew he couldn't please everyone. And many days he didn't. Consequently, he had his share of enemies. But show me a man who has no enemies—and I'll show you a man who has never stood for anything. Bob stood firmly on his beliefs. It is my hope that Bob's successor will have the temperament, tenacity, and vitality to carry on a legacy that few leave behind—that Bob's successor will be a visionary and a beacon for this entire region."

Culver has been replaced by acting county executive John Psota, previously the city manager for the town of Fruitland.

Lewis said that during the first year of Culver's initial term in office, the Wicomico County Sheriff's Office received better pay and benefits, retirement, a disability package for deputies hurt in the line of duty, and a five-year "drop" program for deputies that hadn't even been requested. The drop alternative, which began in Florida for law enforcement officers, firefighters, and other civil servants in the 1980s, allows the employer to contribute a lump sum of money to an account that draws interest if the employee has maximized conventional retirement and wishes to keep working.

The current sheriff's office annual budget is approximately $13 million. Almost two-thirds of the almost 150 employees are sworn personnel with arrest powers. Overall, the sheriff appreciates how much the county council supports his agency, but annual calls for service have risen to approximately forty thousand, requiring nearly four thousand formal criminal investigations.

With that being said, in 2019, Lewis successfully brokered for three new deputies, pointing out that there had been no increase in personnel since he became sheriff.

He noted that the Salisbury and Fruitland police departments were vying for the same pool of law enforcement academy graduates, one of whom fulfilled bi-lingual demands in the jurisdiction: "I have an extremely interested and talented Haitian individual that speaks Creole fluently, and it's something that's been needed in the community for quite some time."

Lewis said he has "gone the extra mile" to hire African Americans and women so they're well represented in the patrol division, criminal investigation unit, and school resource officer cadre. A recent recruit is Pakistani. Lewis is not a proponent of necessarily assigning deputies to neighborhoods comprised of the same race. In his estimation, it is more about the individual officer's ability to relate and be professional.

He is dubious about "implicit bias" training mandated by the state, as it presumes that all white police officers are racists. "I am proud of my deputies who have not bowed down to PC, just as their boss does not. I have not identified one racist officer in my fifteen years here."

The Wicomico County Sheriff's Office was one of fifteen employers out of 2,353 applicants across the nation in 2018 to capture the Freedom Award granted at the Pentagon for unrelenting support of National Guard soldiers and reservists in the agency and the community.

Lewis hailed Corporal Scott Hamilton, a Blackhawk helicopter pilot with the National Guard, and Deputy Anna Bowie and her husband, a state trooper. Deputies are fully paid on deployment in addition to the federal stipend they receive, he said.

"I am just honored to have employees who are dedicated, and I am proud to lead them," said Lewis, who looks forward to displaying the award's American commemorative eagle bust permanently at the new sheriff's office.

Sustaining morale among his deputies is a major priority for Sheriff Lewis. Council members honored four deputies who received medals of valor from the National Sheriffs' Association in 2019.

"It's always a pleasure when we recognize our deputies of their heroic efforts that they do on a daily basis here in Wicomico County," said Lewis, whose office keeps a running tally of salutations. "There were two particular instances that stand out, which caused us to petition the National Sheriffs' Association."

Deputies Howard Bowden and Christian Pecoraro performed "lifesaving measures" on critically injured shooting victims, eliciting valuable information from witnesses and the victims themselves, which resulted in the arrest and prosecution of a murder suspect.

Similar actions by deputies Dylan Miller and Ben Parsons likely saved the life of a man submerged in mud and construction equipment in an overturned van, establishing his breathing airway before fire and rescue personnel arrived to extricate him from the vehicle. "He made a full recovery and was reunited with his family," Lewis said.

Also commended by Lewis and the county council that evening was Tammy Croswell, a thirty-one-year employee of the Wicomico County Emergency Management Center. Croswell's swift tracing of cellular call activity and other useful investigative information dispelled a threat of mass violence at James M. Bennett High School.

The National Sheriffs' Association's annual court security professional award went to Deputy William Oakley in 2013 for supervising the Judicial Protection Unit comprised of eleven sworn personnel and six civilians at the Wicomico County courthouse. The unit handles more than two thousand inmates, ten thousand criminal and civil cases, and two hundred thousand civilians traversing the premises on a yearly basis. In particular, the Wicomico sheriff's deputy efficiently determined which inmates should be kept apart and those deserving protective custody during the most serious, highprofile cases.

Honors have consistently been bestowed upon deputies in the last two years. Sergeant Brian Donohoe received the top award in Region 2 from the National Association of School Resource Officers (NASRO). Sheriff Lewis presented Deputy Dylan Miller with the Mothers Against Drunk Driving Award (MADD) for stellar enforcement of DUI laws in 2020. Miller garnered the same distinction in 2019. Captain Babe Wilson and Sergeant Jeffrey Melvin landed top contributions to the profession and traffic safety commendations, respectively, from the Maryland Sheriffs' Association.

Lewis lauded the retirement of a longtime Wicomico County Sheriff's deputy in a Facebook caption and photo:

"Please join us in congratulating Sergeant Michael Carey who is officially retiring today after thirty-two years of service to the citizens of Wicomico County. We would like to take the opportunity to thank you for your service and we wish you well in your next chapter. Sgt. Carey was presented with his retirement badge and proclamation on behalf of Governor (Larry) Hogan, the State Senate, and the House of Delegates in honor of his service."

A Wicomico County conundrum for Lewis in his formative years as sheriff pertained to a theft ring at the landfill that was far less flattering for county personnel. The aggrieved employee of a large construction company tipped off the sheriff about the alleged improprieties.

Following a community meeting in Pittsville, and based upon information provided by the source, Sheriff Lewis said he stopped a white box truck on US 50 for a mutilated mud flap and failing to display required commercial vehicle identification. Lewis detected the odor of diesel fuel, then discovered five external fuel tanks, each with a hose for siphoning.

The driver of the truck, who worked for Lewis Sand and Gravel (no relation to the sheriff), was arrested. Other arrests ensued, including those of county employees participating in the theft of gasoline and supplies worth tens of thousands of dollars from the landfill. One of them foolishly kept an incriminating diary that documented the lawlessness.

"This case would certainly change the way Wicomico County did business in the future," Lewis said.

In 2017, the Wicomico County Sheriff's Office was one of the first law enforcement agencies on the Eastern Shore to employ both car and body cameras, which coincidentally captured an unfortunate traffic scenario involving a female candidate for county council.

Deputies responded to a car that had apparently veered off the road into a ditch. The lone occupant, Julie Brewington, said she merely pulled over to use her phone. Deputies arrested the blatantly inebriated woman for DUI. Sheriff's records indicate she blamed medication for her condition.

Her social media posts, which were later removed, alleged that she had been mistreated and manhandled by overzealous law enforcement and corrections officers, and threatened to sue. The camera recordings of Ms. Brewington's arrest and booking were played on the national television program Live PD with video evidence rebutting her claims. In addition, Lewis said, she falsely accused him of providing the recordings to the show. "I believe one of the local TV stations did that," he countered.

Aghast viewers posted the following:

> "I think she had about twenty shots of roomertydd arfritis."
>
> "Her lips are stained purple from grate joosth."
>
> "One glass of wine, fifty beers, fourteen shots of vodka."
>
> "I think somebody just drove her car in the ditch as well as her career."
>
> "Julie 'Brew' ington hah. Love a good beer pun."
>
> "Legend has it the woman is still talking."
>
> "If these officers died laughing, would that be considered a homicide?"
>
> "That poor cop took nothing but solid abuse the whole drive to the station. And handled it like a champ. Kudos."
>
> "I was drunk while watching this. I sobered up by the time he finished reading her rights."
>
> "Don't thank the blue enough. Thank you for your service."
>
> "OMG, the sound of the (cell door) shutting in the end was like music to my ears."
>
> "Can't believe she was behind the wheel."

The realtor pled guilty to DUI and was defeated in the election.

According to Sheriff Lewis, "Cameras protect the county from liability and frivolous accusations against deputies."

Cameras vindicated a deputy who was violently assaulted while attempting to arrest a DUI suspect near the Peninsula Regional Medical Center. Miguel Santos's car had jumped over the curb on the road. Recordings of the altercation determined the deputy used justifiable force in self-defense against Santos, who was hospitalized with injuries from the fracas. They also defused a reporter's initial belief that the suspect was wantonly attacked. "I actually thought he (the deputy) used a lot of restraint under the circumstances. He would have looked worse had I been there," Lewis said.

On another occasion featuring camera surveillance, a deputy bodyslammed a drug suspect named Tyrone, who had kicked him in the groin. Reporters rushed to the story, stereotypically assuming "Tyrone" was an African American brutalized by a white cop. They lost interest, Lewis said, when learning that Tyrone was actually white.

"We're capturing any event whether it is a call for service in a home, whether it's approaching a citizen on the street, or whether it is conducting a traffic stop," Sheriff Lewis said.

The Maryland General Assembly passed legislation in 2015 permitting law enforcement agencies to commence pilot bodyworn camera programs. According to the sheriff's office, their implementation is "guided by a policy that incorporates the best practices of the departments around the state that are successfully using this tool. The objectives of body-worn cameras are to enhance deputy safety, facilitate evidentiary integrity, acquire audio and video information, enhance courtroom testimony of proceedings, and assist internal inquiries. Body-worn cameras may also be useful in capturing events such as demonstrations and civil disorder and may be used to provide impartial basis for self-critiques, field evaluations, and recruit deputy training."

The Wicomico County Sheriff's Office also installs cameras in school zones for the purpose of slowing traffic and catching speeders.

Unlike money allocated to the state from citations issued by patrol deputies, revenue from camera-generated tickets remains in Wicomico County. Local drivers were at first irritated by the cameras, according to Lewis, but have mostly become conditioned to their utility in the name of public safety.

Effective leadership, he remarked, "is being empathetic and sympathetic, but you must stand up for the values of the community in which you serve."

Leading by example is a key dimension, continued the sheriff who still makes traffic stops in his black, unmarked SUV after fifteen years in office and responds directly to major crime scenes.

He recently ticketed a motorist from Hebron driving 102 miles an hour on US 13, even passing people on the shoulder of the road. True to form, Lewis knew the father and grandfather of the man, who had likely been smoking marijuana.

Sheriff Lewis pulled over a fellow who appeared to be talking on his cell phone while driving but claimed to be listening to music. Thanks to being polite, the driver received a warning from him. Later the same day, the individual contacted the sheriff to say he had lied about not using the phone and wanted to be cited because of teaching his children to tell the truth. Lewis respected the man's candor, saying he was acutely aware of what was actually going on. No citation was issued.

"One of the toughest things is when I stop someone with kids in the car for a traffic violation and the kids want to cut up and have a photo taken with me," said the sheriff, whose desire to know Wicomico County residents on a more personal level is emboldened by serving a somewhat smaller community.

There are advantages and disadvantages of being an extroverted leader, according to Lewis: "You can capture the attention at a crime scene or in front of an audience. But you can offend people quickly when your words carry a lot of weight in the office. I try to choose my words carefully with a certain segment of the electorate. They have the opportunity to unelect me."

According to Cannon, Sheriff Lewis exudes "self-confidence and humility; gregarious by nature, but quite formidable when necessary, a complex combination of attributes necessary when establishing a strong foundation of virtuous leadership."

Lewis realizes that some of his younger road deputies assume that he merely reads the paper each morning in his office, drinks a leisurely cup of coffee, and chats with his command staff. "I don't have time for that," he explained. "We are putting out fires from the time I come in, from the time I walk through that [office] door until I go to bed at night."

With his versatile background and myriad contacts, he has been known to orchestrate investigations and arrests of felons from his office. An example was the apprehension near the Susquehanna Bridge in Harford County of Lamir Dasham Elam, a North Carolina murder suspect.

"I applaud the Duplin County, North Carolina, Sheriff's Office for promptly calling me and allowing me to coordinate the traffic stop with the Maryland state troopers on I-95. This exemplifies teamwork in getting a deadly and dangerous criminal off the streets while bringing some closure to the family of our victims. It was our pleasure to assist all of Duplin County."

His reputation in criminal justice circles was highlighted when Beau Oglesby, now a circuit court judge, ran successfully for Worcester County State's Attorney with a sterling Fraternal Order of Police endorsement: "Beau Oglesby was the chief prosecutor in many of Sheriff Lewis's drug cases when Sheriff Lewis was a state trooper. He was recognized by Wicomico County Drug Task force for outstanding efforts in prosecuting drug deals and asset forfeiture."

A renowned guru in police tactics, Lewis's opinion about the fatal police shooting of a wheelchair-bound man in Wilmington, Delaware, was solicited by reporters. After wounding himself, the twenty-eight year-old refused to raise his hands and drop the gun, ostensibly posing a threat to bystanders and law enforcement.

"Cemeteries are full of police officers across the country who hesitated to pull the trigger and were waiting for the suspect to shoot first," he said. "Consequently, they lost their lives."

The sheriff considers himself a man of principle. He generally "enjoys" people, confessing that his "weakest strength" is the inability to say no. In particular, he believes in helping too often forgotten crime victims, as the criminal justice process caters more to perpetrators.

"I have seen him go to the store, load up a trunk full of presents and give them to families who suffered a loss," Maciarello said. "He loved them [the victims], comforted them, he would continue to look upon them, visit with them; his service to victims during my time as State's Attorney never, ever seemed to have an end."

Lewis exclaimed, "I represent everyone regardless of race, gender, or politics. If you don't know where I stand by now, something is wrong. I won't change who I am." Lewis repeated that "surrendering" to "woke" political correctness is not on the table.

"If you're trying to make everyone happy in this position, you're not doing your job. There will be people who don't like what you say and do. Every decision I make is in the best interest of the county and the agency," he said. "When I was elected, I made it clear we were going from a more reactive to a more proactive agency. That we were changing the way things were done. We have given (the deputies) the tools they need."

"Mike Lewis was and is the real deal when it comes to defining a top cop—a leader through and through, who day in and day out, leads by example," Senator Carozza said.

He understands that all people, including his deputies, make mistakes. "If you are doing your job for the right reasons and something goes wrong, I will have your back."

Officers can also be subjected to litigation. Deputy Benjamin Parsons, Corporal Cristan Taylor, and two Delmar police officers were accused of excessive force in a lawsuit filed on behalf of Marcus Bounds. Reports indicated that Bounds, found by Parsons slumped over the steering wheel of his car in a stupor, was charged with DWI and resisting arrest after being tased three times in a wild altercation.

The United States Court of Appeals ruled in favor of the deputies and police officers: "As the district court acknowledged, the video tape of the occurrence filmed at night and from a distance, is not of perfect quality and it is not unambiguous in all respects. But taken together, the record evidence, in this case, puts beyond genuine dispute that Bounds, at a minimum, was physically resistant and noncompliant with officer instructions."

Another affront to dedicated law enforcement officers is impersonation. One individual, Lewis said, worked security for years at the hospital. When deputies were unable to locate the suspect, Lewis noticed in the *Daily Times* that there was a wake scheduled for a relative of the man. He personally arrested him at Holloway Funeral Home. In a second scenario, according to Lewis, a Salisbury firefighter was charged with impersonation when he flashed a bogus police badge at a deputy who pulled him over for speeding in Mardela Springs. The vehicle, which resembled an unmarked patrol cruiser, had been used to stop motorists and housed 250 rounds of ammunition.

Unfortunately, a disappointing situation for law enforcement prompted the resignation of Deputy Joel Arnold in 2009. He was charged with second-degree assault, reckless endangerment, false imprisonment, and malicious destruction of property concerning a domestic altercation at a Canvasback Court residence. An internal investigation by the sheriff's office verified Arnold's culpability. The victim, his live-in girlfriend, and a fellow sheriff's deputy, refused to testify against him.

Rebutting acidic remarks in cyberspace that stereotyped law enforcement and lambasted the sheriff, a blogger wrote: "Police work is inherently dangerous and causes a great deal of stress on people. That is why most of the population does not choose to do police work. Some people would like total anarchy. The sheriff cannot control the actions of an individual in an off-duty capacity nor should he be held accountable for them. People, if in police work, or a doctor, or a telephone repairman, do things randomly. The majority of all police officers are dedicated professionals."

Like most of the world, Lewis and his deputies coped with the madness of the COVID-19 outbreak in 2020. The mandates and protocols of Maryland Governor Larry Hogan and Lori Brewster, director of the Wicomico County Health Department, fluctuated with the unpredictability of the ailment.

Two men were arrested by deputies, for instance, at a home on South Westover Drive for hosting a loud party of twenty-five revelers, violating Hogan's stay-at-home order and his executive order allowing no more than ten people per gathering.

The sheriff's office discontinued "proactive enforcement" the first four weeks of the pandemic to decrease the odds of human interaction and contamination, something "common criminals" capitalized on, according to Lewis. "We had to get back to being proactive because the public deserved it."

The COVID-19 hysteria increased the number of burglaries and domestic assaults, Lewis said. Landlords battled to evict tenants who were ten to twelve months behind on their rent as the economy sputtered.

Deputies wearing masks, gloves, and protective garments were sweating profusely in the summer heat.

Not only were sheriff's deputies sporting masks, so were miscreants conveniently concealing their identities committing crimes and, in the national spectrum, societal unrest. Donning masks became a trademark of the domestic terrorist organization Antifa that blatantly ignored social distancing.

Ironically, the year prior to COVID-19, witnesses were readily able to identify the alleged robber of the PNC Bank on North Salisbury Boulevard because he wasn't wearing a mask. Task force members arrested him in the parking lot of the Food Lion on Snow Hill Road.

COVID-19 has made it much more difficult to process prisoners at central booking of the Wicomico County Detention Center, Lewis explained, as district court commissioners busily schedule arraignments and first appearances. More summonses for court appearances are being issued than arrest warrants, also enabling criminals.

Lewis understands why deputies avoid direct contact under perilous circumstances with certain civilians for fear they could contract the virus and take it home to their families. "I have to hope they make good choices."

Waffling COVID-19 precautions, deemed a politically preposterous hot potato by some people, separated band students at Washington state's Wenatchee High School in green, inflatable "sci-fi" capsules that looked fully capable of levitating to another planet.

Sheriff Lewis, like so many leaders around the nation, considers COVID-19 uncharted territory that compels flexibility and patience contingent upon jurisdictional provisions and needs.

The primary law enforcement inspiration for Lewis has been David B. Mitchell, former Maryland State Police superintendent and now chief of the University of Maryland police department. Mitchell was also director of Homeland Security in Delaware and retired as

Prince Georges County police chief.

"He was confident and sincere," traits Lewis appreciated while working for Mitchell as a state trooper. "He was appointed by the governor and was never a trooper himself, but he made it clear he would need to earn our respect. He commanded respect, but he did not demand it."

Superintendent Mitchell always wore the Maryland State Police uniform and Stetson hat rather than a suit and tie, a meaningful statement about authority, the trooper culture, and training, an approach Lewis transitioned to the sheriff's office. "One of my tough sells at first was requiring deputies to wear the Stetson hat to build a professional law enforcement image. They must be worn in public while on duty."

And Lewis never forgot that Mitchell flew over to the Peninsula Regional Medical Center from the Western Shore to visit critically wounded trooper Kevin Plank before he expired.

Edward T. Norris also makes Lewis's list of admirable people. Lewis, Rudy Giuliani, and former governor Ehrlich requested a presidential pardon of Norris, who served time in federal prison for misappropriation of slush funds, that was not granted by President Trump in his waning hours at the White House.

Norris was deputy commissioner of the New York Police Department on Mayor Giuliani's watch, applauded for his data drive, com-stat formula that prioritized police presence and enforcement and lowered crime rates. He endorsed the "broken window" theory, Lewis said, that the "big things" (serious offenses) can only be reduced by fixing the "small things" that spread urban blight and hopelessness.

Lewis said Norris was a tough, "no-nonsense" cop who engendered respect among the rank and file at NYPD.

Then-mayor Martin O'Malley hired Norris as the police commissioner in Baltimore, where crime rates also dropped. Governor Ehrlich soon lured him to become superintendent of the Maryland State Police, something O'Malley resented deeply, in Lewis's opinion.

Sheriff Lewis said the political drama persisted when O'Malley defeated Ehrlich for the governorship and orchestrated a retaliatory witch hunt that resulted in Norris's incarceration.

The US attorney general indicted Norris on three charges, alleging illegal expenditures of over $20,000 derived from the Baltimore Police Department's supplemental account for personal gifts and women he allegedly courted in extramarital affairs. Norris was sentenced to six months in federal prison, six months of home detention, and five hundred hours of community service.

He presently hosts the Ed Norris Show on FM radio in Baltimore.

Political bloodletting and jurisdictional schisms are common among law enforcement ranks, pitting counties against municipalities and local agencies often perceiving state police as aloof and uncommunicative, a shortcoming Lewis experienced as a trooper and strives to mitigate.

Lewis has been asked, in fact, whether he prefers consolidating local law enforcement agencies under the purview of the sheriff's office. "I would be receptive to the idea, as long as the sheriff is elected rather than appointed. But most municipal jurisdictions don't want to give up their authority and autonomy," said the former president of the Maryland Sheriffs' Association, adding that his agency has crafted productive, generally seamless rapport with the Salisbury and Fruitland police departments.

The sheriff credited incoming Salisbury police chief Barbara Duncan with fueling cooperation, "unlike her predecessor (Allan Webster)." The Wicomico County Sheriff's Office is mandated to propagate all protective orders, peace orders, evictions, warrants, and criminal summonses in the Salisbury city limits.

Teamwork was in play when the Wicomico County Sheriff's Office Community Action Team obtained a seizure and search warrant leading to the arrest of Detrick Butler on various firearms, narcotics trafficking, possession with intent to distribute, and drug manufacturing charges.

Records indicate the Salisbury police tactical unit discovered a shed on the property dedicated to manufacturing crack cocaine with two Pyrex dishes, cutting devices, alcohol, and other germane utensils. Also seized from the Shamrock Avenue residence were powder cocaine, marijuana, nearly $4,000 cash, and two semi-automatic handguns.

Lewis worried that information sharing and intel among jurisdictions was endangered in early 2021 because the FBI's transition from UCR (Uniform Crime Reporting) to NIBRS (National Incident Based Reporting System) omitted nearly one-quarter of local law enforcement agencies in America from punctually submitting crime data.

Even though the Wicomico County Sheriff's Office is active in the new NIBRS, Lewis said: "I find it (the data deficit) very troublesome. We want a discernible picture of crime going on across the country, especially when it comes to attacks on law enforcement officers." Memorandums of Understanding (MOU's) certify overlapping geographical arrest powers among law enforcement agencies in certain portions of the community and elsewhere. For example, reacting to the late-night muggings perpetrated against college students, the Salisbury University Police Department extended its reach along a stretch of South Salisbury Boulevard that had been patrolled exclusively by the Wicomico County Sheriff's Office and the Maryland State Police.

Another MOA (Memorandum of Agreement) unified the Wicomico County Sheriff's Office, the Salisbury Police Department, the Wicomico County Child Advocacy Center, the Wicomico County State's Attorney's Office, and the Life Crisis Center through mutual information sharing and resources in the fight to mitigate maltreatment of children and their families.

A resolution was approved in 2020 by the Wicomico County Council forging a mutual aid agreement among all sheriff's offices and county governments on the Eastern Shore. Lewis said the resources and personnel could be especially vital "should we experience civil disorder resulting in rioting and looting. Passing the MOU provides these counties with blanket security and enables their men and women to assist one another."

Worcester County Sheriff Matt Crisafulli echoed the enthusiasm, praising the MRAP for its capabilities in mass casualty situations and major breaches of the law, the sheriff said.

Lewis guaranteed the support of the Wicomico Sheriff's Office during the H20i "pop-up" car rallies causing havoc in Ocean City. Riots broke out in the spring of 2020, and the fall mayhem produced more than 1,500 citations and 121 arrests, with a state trooper being knocked unconscious by a suspect.

"This is not a car show, and the majority of these visitors are not car enthusiasts," lamented Ocean City Police Chief Ross Buzzuro. "They are here to disrupt, destroy, and disrespect our community and our law enforcement officers."

MOUs are not confined to Wicomico County or the state of Maryland. After signing a pact with a county in Georgia, the enterprising Lewis seized $327,000 on a traffic stop in 2019 from a drug runner who confessed that the money was derived from the sale of hashish and marijuana. The suspect was planning to smuggle the proceeds through the Atlanta airport on his way back to California. In a separate arrest, Lewis and the local sheriff confiscated the first kilo of methamphetamine in the area.

Mutual cooperation, however, momentarily afflicted the response of the Wicomico County Sheriff's Office, Salisbury Police Department, and the Salisbury University Police Department to a murder-suicide in 2013 at off-campus housing only three blocks from the school. Shortly past 6 p.m., law enforcement received reports of a shooting in an area known as "the zoo" because of typical college parties and shenanigans. After drinking a bottle of vodka and driving one hour to Salisbury, Ryan Shallue forcibly entered the residence, critically wounded former girlfriend and Salisbury University student

Kristen Loetz, killed her male companion Charles Abbott, and then fatally shot himself.

In what the Salisbury *Daily Times* headlined "Blurred Boundaries," there was initial confusion about whether the residence sat in the county or city limits until tax records confirmed the former, compelling the sheriff's office to lead the investigation. "I didn't care whose jurisdiction it was," Lewis said. "I immediately assumed control of the crime scene."

Lewis said Shallue had stalked Loetz and texted her often since their break-up four months earlier. They argued briefly at the house, and when Abbott tried to intervene, the assailant pulled out a handgun and began shooting.

University President Janet Dudley-Eshbach and her public relations team scrambled to figure out how to be informative and above board without panicking students and faculty who were on campus for night classes. "School shootings" were also posing a public relations nightmare for colleges and universities around the country.

The previous year, the president and her police chief, Edwin Lashley, held a forum regarding campus security and emergency management.

Fewer than two hundred faculty, staff, and administrators attended. The higher education culture of openness, a certain resistance to authority, and the ongoing assumption that unconscionable violence only occurs elsewhere have too often conspired against more stringent measures to safeguard lives and property.

While the sheriff's office swiftly notified the public that a shooting on Onley Road had occurred, no message emanated from the university until approximately 7:45, with students receiving erroneous texts from friends in the interim that the shooter was on his way to campus. It was a lesson learned for the university about timely messaging to frightened and displeased students expecting instantaneous social media affirmation. The school did not go into lockdown, either, something it rectified weeks later when a suspected drug dealer drove his truck over the hood of a state police cruiser one mile away from downtown and fled on foot in the direction of Salisbury University. Three undercover officers inside the vehicle fired at thirty-one-year-old Edwin Fletcher in self-defence.

Lewis emphasized that "enhancements in physical security" are being refined for universities and K through 12 for "increased awareness and collaboration between school and local law enforcement personnel about emergency plans, building access control, classroom door locks, barriers to deter hostile intruders, and emergency notification systems."

With a gaggle of reporters congregating at the scene of the murder suicide, Sheriff Lewis convened a press conference as lead spokesperson flanked by the president, university police chief, and the state's attorney. "By holding it there, we wanted to be transparent and let people know the area was secured. The entire community and the school had been traumatized by what happened," said Lewis, whose daughter was a Salisbury University freshman at the time.

Ms. Loetz, the survivor of the shooting and an honors student in the nursing program, rebounded bravely to deliver the keynote address at Salisbury University's commencement.

An embarrassing scenario unfolded at Salisbury University in 2020 when the former president of the Student Government Association was arrested by sheriff's detectives on six sex offense charges.

Snapchat messages transmitted by Brendan Link allegedly solicited a sixteen-year-old boy for pornography and sex acts, including recording trysts with girls that could be sold for profit. Deputies, who executed search warrants in two homes and on numerous electronic devices, began the probe because the boy's mother complained about Link.

The university emitted a tepid statement following inquiries about the arrest: "SU does not comment on legal issues faced by individual students. I can confirm, however, that Brendan Link is currently enrolled at SU. He was elected as Student Government Association president in April and resigned in July."

The Wicomico County Sheriff's Office participated in another investigation that placed the university under the microscope in the racially incendiary national narrative. Between September 2019 and early 2020, racist graffiti was discovered on four occasions in classroom buildings on campus. The messages contained slurs, depictions of hangings, and an ominous reference to the Sandy Hook mass shooting.

Most of the school and general public were not alerted of the graffiti until February, at which time outraged president Charles Wight issued a statement excoriating the behavior: "Not one but multiple racist threats are being directed at Black and Brown members of OUR community. An attack on some members of our campus community is an attack on all of us."

The campus's NAACP (National Association for the Advancement of Colored People) chapter tweeted a photo of the vandalism. The Change SU Coalition was formed. A protest in the college square attracted around two hundred people at a school enrolling approximately 8,500 students.

President Wight canceled classes for a "day of healing," noting that the counseling center, diversity and inclusion office, and multicultural student services would remain open should traumatized students desire assistance.

In March, authorities said a suspect had been "identified" in the case, pleasing the president. "The racist threats on the walls and doors of the university's academic buildings caused a great deal of fear," Wight said. "We hope this development in the investigation helps to bring a sense of security to the school."

The FBI had entered the probe, but months elapsed with no arrests, charges, or updates, sustaining speculation, bewilderment, and skepticism on and off campus.

That finally changed in June when Jerome Kevin Jackson, a fifty-four-year-old grandfather of five, was adjudicated guilty of maliciously defacing property in connection with incidents of racist and threatening graffiti. Judge Abigail March sentenced Jackson to eighteen months rather than the maximum of three years in the Wicomico County Detention Center following his plea deal conceding culpability.

Hours of recorded video surveillance confirmed that Jackson, an African American from Princess Anne, had acted alone.

The prosecutor extracted no silver lining from Jackson's crimes: "Mr. Jackson wielded a very heavy hammer, and that hammer was filled with racism; that hammer was filled with hate."

Jackson's wife graduated from the college.

A decline in enrollment was generally blamed on the fallout and adverse publicity from the graffiti. SU administrators and the public relations office fielded countless complaints and concerns during the ordeal, indignant donors threatened to spend their money elsewhere, and a six-figure diversity and inclusion chief was hired the same summer despite conjecture about supposed funding deficits caused by the pandemic.

"I was disgusted by the university's response and the politics that quickly played a role in the case," Sheriff Lewis said. "I knew early on there was an African American male involved in the case, and they (the school) allowed racial divisiveness and bigotry around the country to delay getting the facts out quickly. Shame on SU."

He lauded the Salisbury University Police Department and its lead female detective, though, for doing an "excellent job" of assessing what transpired.

Eerily similar graffiti was perpetrated in the new university library several years prior by two male African American students who were verbally reprimanded without being expelled or charged.

Drowning in racial animosity, the school attracted unwanted exposure from endangered conservative national media in 2018 when education professor Erin Stutelberg was teaching the elements of a

"White Supremacy Pyramid" that ran the gamut from genocide to microaggressions.

A communication arts colleague who criticized the prejudice of the pyramid was admonished by the provost and ordered to meet with his department chair and dean for disciplinary purposes.

Social media posts reflected perceived media hijinks and reverse discrimination in Mr. Jackson's graffiti caper:

> "The MSN stations will not report this. It doesn't fit their narrative. Now, let me look up 'egg on your face' to share with the SU president and Salisbury mayor."
>
> "Need racism for your displays of moral superiority? Blame a white, frame a white. I blame liberals, not blacks."
>
> "If he was white and Republican, their names would already be in the New York Times and Washington Post. The (Salisbury) Daily Times wouldn't have a font size large enough in their emotional and breathless attacks on 'racist and bigoted Trump supporters.' SU students would be crying and pleading for 'justice' and would be marching the streets, protesting the racist hillbillies and telling everyone how afraid they are of even walking the streets anymore."
>
> "Graffiti Artist Named As New SU Dean of Diversity."
>
> "Everyone from the SU president's office, Jake Day's office, the SU Black Student Union, and the majority of SU faculty were convinced, and wanted this to be a white person."
>
> *sbynews.blogspot.com*

The following passage is from "The fallacy of unfettered freedom and indispensable inclusion" message to Salisbury University liberal arts faculty articulated by the author of this book upon his retirement from the school: "Faculty should eschew shamelessly subjecting students to partisan ideology and political agendas betraying any semblance of tolerance, let alone Socratic learning. The worst affront to academic discourse, perhaps, is that certain faculty are too compliant or intimidated" to convey sentiments offending the national narrative permeating higher education "for fear of condemnation or retaliation concerning tenure, promotion, and general job satisfaction."

Unharnessed cancel culture is apparently invading the ivory tower in various capacities. Jodi Shaw left her staff position at prestigious Smith College in Massachusetts after being subjected to heavyhanded race training and shaming, even though video and audio surveillance refuted an alleged "racial" incident that occurred in the dining hall. "This kind of behavior is illiberal. It's very dogmatic and rigid ideology, and authoritarian," said Shaw, who was also precluded from performing rap music for being a white woman committing "cultural appropriation."

While the underpinnings of "social justice" on college campuses were already affixed, schools aggressively contrived mechanisms for protecting students from the emotional "horrors" of Donald Trump's election in 2016. "As college and university administrators went into crisis mode, they sought to provide students with spaces to relieve their post-electoral anxiety and distress. Safe spaces have been provided with coloring books, crayons, therapy pets, and even pacifiers. They have come to most resemble pediatric units," said Michael Rectenwald, a New York University professor.

In addition to controversy at Salisbury and other universities, there are worries about the general breakdown of societal norms that impacts K through 12 public schools. No doubt, people of Sheriff Lewis's generation could never have imagined the necessity for armed law enforcement resource officers and security devices in public schools where unhinged, rebellious students from frequently fragmented families intimidate teachers and administrators.

School Resource Officers (SROs) began sporadically in the 1950s, including an attempt to develop rapport between police and students in Flint, Michigan. The early SROs were counselors, coaches, tutors, and mentors. By the 1980s, they often wore uniforms and started carrying weapons. The Gun-Free Schools Act of 1994 heightened their presence as juvenile crime and gang members further disrupted the learning environment. By 2000, the Department of Justice allocated $750 million to the Cops in School grants program that facilitated hiring more than 6,500 school resource officers around the nation.

The contemporary SRO is frequently a jack-of-all-trades balancing an enforcement role, deterrence, and stimulating relationships with students that ostensibly motivate mutual understanding and a more upbeat opinion of law enforcement.

Wicomico sheriff's resource officer Ryan Osterwalder's investigation was crucial to the prosecution of sixteen-year-old Daquan Parks in the ugly assault of assistant principal Lisa Forbush and the principal, Rick Briggs, at James M. Bennett High School in 2016. Sheriff's reports indicate that Parks became enraged when he was told to stay in the main hallway before the first bell rang for class. He pushed Forbush over a counter and tried to choke her, knocked the intervening Briggs to the ground with a flurry of punches, and had to be restrained by other school personnel.

The victims were transported to Peninsula Regional Medical Center for injuries sustained in the attack. The Fruitland teenager was tried as an adult, receiving a ten-year sentence with five years suspended on convictions of first-degree assault, second-degree assault, and disorderly conduct.

The next year at Bennett, the school resource officer was essential to mitigating a brawl that ignited several fights on campus and resulted in numerous arrests. Responding law enforcement officers used pepper spray to quell the uprising, and the school went on lockdown. "We had one hell of a mess over there," remembered Lewis about the bedlam.

Disciplining students has become increasingly difficult terrain, inviting litigation. After witnessing recorded surveillance video, Wicomico County Sheriff's Office school resource officer Appellee Dolgos detained a girl who had kicked and pummeled a classmate on a moving school bus. Dolgos reported the assailant emitted no contrition or concern for what happened as she spoke to her and Salisbury Elementary School administrators. She reminded the child that adults would be jailed for equivalent conduct.

Based on the gravity of the assault and potential volatility, the school resource officer of ten years briefly handcuffed the girl, who began crying, complaining the cuffs were too tight, and apologizing.

She was turned over to her mother, and a lawsuit filed by Salisbury attorney Robin Cockey against the Wicomico County Sheriff's Office followed. It alleged unreasonable seizure and excessive force under the Fourth Amendment, battery, and assault. The court deemed the plaintiffs failed to prove the deputy acted with malice or gross negligence, the same decision rendered by an appellate circuit judge.

A passage from the second court ruling, however, alluded to the contemporary challenges of balancing restraint with troubled children in today's educational maelstrom and the need for discipline in public schools:

> "School-based policing is the fastest growing area of law enforcement. While the officers' presence surely keeps the nation's children safe, officers should not handcuff young students who have committed minor offenses but do not pose an immediate threat to safety and will not evade arrest. Unnecessarily handcuffing and criminally punishing young school children is undoubtedly humiliating, scarring, and emotionally damaging. We must be mindful of the longlasting impact such actions have on these children and their ability to flourish and lead productive lives."

In 2018, school resource officer Blake Gaskill confronted seventeenyear-old gunman Austin Rollins in the hallway at Great Mills High School in southern Maryland across the Chesapeake Bay from Wicomico County. Rollins had just killed his ex-girlfriend Jaelynn Willey and wounded another student. Gaskill fired a bullet that struck the Glock pistol wielded by Rollins as the suspect fatally shot himself in the head.

The sheriff's office supplies all school resource officers to Wicomico County's public schools. In 2019, 85% of "juvenile referrals" by the sheriff's office were generated by SRO's.

Lewis said he "will fight to the very end" pending legislation in Maryland to eliminate school resources officers from K through 12 and prohibit response to school emergencies by patrol deputies in their formal uniforms. "I can't imagine if we did not have deputies embedded in schools. What would happen to the educators and good students who want to learn?"

School safety is a component of community policing consistently advocated by Sheriff Lewis and other law enforcement officials to address fear, hostility, and communication barriers in Wicomico County.

Anti-drug education programs including DARE (Drug Abuse Resistance Education) have proliferated nationally along with recreational initiatives like PAL (Police Athletic League), engaging teens and children, bicycle patrols, small business incentives, building codes, neighborhood watch, schools, non-for-profit, and media organizations partnering with other stakeholders that seemingly contradict myopic public perceptions of actual police obligations. In truth, "social work" is strongly synonymous with law enforcement.

Automobiles, telecommunication, and suburbanization distanced police officers who once "walked the beat" from connecting with the populace. Community policing, also known as COP (Community Orienting Policing), gained traction in the 1960s with Lyndon Johnson's President's Commission and Law Enforcement Administration of Justice, aiming to reduce the disconnect between police and the citizenry, especially in minority neighborhoods.

The fledgling Wicomico County Explorer Post 451 program, sponsored and organized by the sheriff's office, holds meetings for area youth interested in law enforcement and criminal justice careers. Their initial project collected new socks before Christmas of 2020 for shelters such as Halo and Joseph House. Explored Post 451 advances the importance of being a positive and respectful citizen of the community.

Community policing endeavors to preempt more dangerous, disrespectful behavior such as the "Jungle" video on YouTube that reportedly featured young local males pointing handguns at the camera and motioning as if they were about to fire them at the viewer, with the threat "we kickin' in your front door." The piece was eventually removed from the site.

Lewis said the Crips, MS-13, the Bloods, and Bloods affiliate Tree Top Piru are among the gangs functioning in Wicomico County, with heavy spillover from the crime-infested Baltimore area. According to Lewis, some gang bangers are lured and emboldened because of spineless urban leadership. In Virginia, "politically correct" authorities have curtailed buckling down on gangs because of "discriminatory" enforcement, he added.

Notorious Tree Top Piru Bloods leader Sherman Pride of Salisbury, also known as Dark Black and DB, garnered 292 months in prison for narcotics trafficking, conspiracy to commit murder, and robbery in a crackdown that also put several associates behind bars. Pride maintained Bloods connections in Baltimore, where one of his comrades was producing "Stop Snitching" videos on social media to terrify anyone perceived as treasonous.

The Bloods were founded in the early 1970s in Los Angeles. Many members of the gang have been recruited from the revolving door of prison inmates.

Nonetheless, comprehensive community policing has evolved over the years to deter the criminal element from gaining traction in vulnerable neighborhoods. In Manatee County, Florida, for instance,

"Operation Facelift" implemented by Sheriff Charles B. Wells mirrored the "broken windows" concept advanced by one of Lewis's favorites, Ed Norris, in New York City and Baltimore to tackle core poverty and family dysfunction that breeds crime.

In 1994, the Clinton administration established the Office of Community Oriented Policing funded through the Department of Justice with mixed results. Grant money gradually spawned community policing teams that also reached smaller towns and outlying areas.

Community policing is sometimes criticized for being expensive and "touchy-feely," deflecting officers from more urgent crime-fighting realities. Detractors argue social obedience and quality of life must be sustained by the community itself, not merely the police, and that it is delusional to believe officers should be "friends" with everyone they encounter.

An essential variable of community policing, the effectiveness of which remains difficult to assess quantitatively, is that officers become intimately familiar with neighborhoods by cultivating rapport. In theory, it enables police to determine the needs of law-abiding citizens while collecting intel about common criminals and gangs.

There are several neighborhood associations in Wicomico County that appeal to conscientious residents comparing notes on crime, housing maintenance, code enforcement, traffic and parking concerns, and general quality of life. The University Neighborhood Association, for example, has been active on social media platforms, produces a newsletter, and meets regularly.

"We know how important volunteers can be. A great resource for my deputies is the eyes and ears of the community members we serve. I welcome citizens patrols in the neighborhoods. We must harness the power of every individual," Lewis said.

The sheriff's office holds meetings each year with neighborhood groups and town-gown stakeholders through the university, along with the communities of Hebron, Mardela Springs, Sharptown, Pittsville, and Willards.

In 2019, the sheriff's office delivered 232 peace orders and protective orders, mechanisms for preserving domestic and neighborhood tranquility. Maryland State Police reports reveal that fifty-yearold Sharon Kohlhoff of Sharptown had inquired about obtaining a protective order before fatally shooting her husband, Edward Kohlhoff, but did not request further assistance. She was charged with first-degree murder.

A traditional facet of community policing is crime prevention, enabling deputies to advise homeowners, businesses, and other entities about burglar alarms, the best locks for doors and windows, security cameras, personal safety, and more.

Disaster drills are conducted by the Wicomico County Sheriff's Office with various organizations, including Salisbury University and the Salisbury-Ocean City Regional Airport. In 2017, the sheriff's office began offering free training for civilians, especially businesses and places of worship, to combat active shooters.

Sergeant Brian Donohoe received an award for crime prevention excellence from the Maryland Sheriffs' Association in 2020.

Crime prevention measures paid off at a Mardela Springs home.

Not only did the alarm activate, but camera surveillance positively identified Jamie Ruark and Warren Christopher Parker as the burglars after deputies discovered an open window and pry marks on the front door.

A security camera in the university residential area captured a teenager in 2020 returning to admire an elderly man's car he had deliberately burned. Authorities charged the fourteen-year-old, who lived a block away, for a second act of vehicle arson as well.

Video surveillance also precipitated the arrest of two young men who burglarized the Wicomico Youth and Civic Center where COVID-19 vaccinations were being administered, according to the sheriff's office.

Tragically, personal safety tips did not prevent seven-year-old Dylan Joseph Wheatley of Mardela Springs, who aspired to be a police officer, from dying when his off-road ATV pulled out in front of an oncoming car. He was transported to PRMC in critical condition and expired a short time later.

But heartening community interaction with law enforcement followed: his mother, Vicki Wheatley, donated a protective vest in Dylan's memory to "Rookie," a K–9 with the sheriff's office.

Lewis said the timing was impeccable given that two K–9's had been shot in the United States the same week. "Building a resilient community involves multiple sectors and meaningful engagement from every corner of our society."

The importance of partnering was displayed when sheriff's deputies retrieved an injured bald eagle on Yacht Club Road and transported it to the Salisbury Zoo for treatment. The bird, estimated to be three years old by zoo officials and unable to fly, made a successful recovery.

"We are out to save every life. We do the job whether it is helping the community or our feathered friends," said Lieutenant Robinson while lauding the efforts of the zoo.

"At a time when many people are feeling contrary, I am still optimistic about the future of law enforcement and community relations," Lewis said.

He and State's Attorney Maciarello reveled in the annual Read Across America event at the Wicomico County Library. The first seventy-five children in attendance received free books for the special occasion that is held in February to commemorate Dr. Seuss's birthday.

In 2020, "No Shave November" enabled deputies to shelve their razors and collect $200,000 in donations from sheriff's office personnel for support, prevention, research, and education devoted to the local American Cancer Society-Relay for Life.

Just before Christmas the same year, the Wicomico County Sheriff's Office bonded with Perdue Transportation, Bikers Without Borders, the Patriot Guard, and the American Legion Riders to carry wreaths for display at the Delaware Veterans Memorial Cemetery in Millsboro.

The sheriff's office is a sponsor of the annual Seagull Century at Salisbury University, one of the largest bicycle rides in America. Other recent civic engagement includes the Unity and NAACP rallies, the MADD (Mothers Against Drunk Driving) impact panel, and Operation We Care in conjunction with the Wicomico County Health

Department.

Operation We Care was founded in 2007 by business owners Jeff and Diana Merritt of Salisbury. The group arranges donations and care packages for area law enforcement agencies and local residents serving in the military. OWC, VFW Post 194, and Whole Roast Barbeque Services provided lunches to Wicomico County sheriff's deputies Valentine's weekend of 2021, sustaining the community connection that contradicts negativity about law enforcement.

Haven P. Simmons

CHAPTER THREE

SARAH'S SAGA AND HORRENDOUS HUMAN AFFLICTIONS

The Sarah Foxwell case was the most heart-wrenching in Sheriff Mike Lewis's law enforcement career. "She was lying on her back with her little arms reached out to the sky to heaven," Lewis recounted despondently.

"I was physically and emotionally void of any meaningful response other than sobbing with those around me," Lewis said.

Sarah Haley Foxwell, known as "Haley Bug" by her family, was a perpetually smiling, outgoing sixth-grader, the middle of nine children raised predominantly by a single mother.

In December 2009, however, the eleven-year-old was living with her grandmother and younger sister in a converted barn house.

The weather dipped below freezing, and it was snowing as the sun set over the Maryland Eastern Shore three days before Christmas. Sarah and her six-year-old sister went to bed at around 9 p.m. in the room they shared at the end of the hallway next to the back of the home.

Early the following morning, Sarah was nowhere to be found. Only her green toothbrush was missing. The family called Sarah's mother, who notified the Wicomico County Sheriff's Office.

According to sheriff's office investigative files, deputies responded to the house with Sheriff Lewis fearing the child may have been kidnapped. "Every deputy at this office came back to work. They didn't want to spend Christmas with their families knowing this little girl was missing," said Lewis, who promised the mother he would do everything possible to bring Sarah home.

There was no sign of forced entry, deputies ascertained. The front door and windows were locked, but not the back door. They learned the dog hadn't barked in the night. Also revealing was the fact that a key hidden outside for emergencies was gone, meaning the culprit was likely familiar with the property and knew his way around.

It wasn't long before investigators found out that the younger sister had told her grandmother that she pretended to be asleep but saw the man take Sarah from the bedroom after he said vile things to her. The sister also reportedly told her mother that "Tommy took her." An Amber Alert was activated.

"Tommy" was Thomas Leggs, a convicted pedophile and the former boyfriend of Sarah's Aunt Amy. He had served six months of a seven-year sentence for the fourth-degree rape of a teenager and was adjudicated guilty of committing a third-degree sex offense against a child. Leggs was out on bond after being arrested again for assaulting a young woman in an eerily similar scenario a few months earlier.

"He crawled through the window in the middle of the night, and she saw him standing there with his clothing on the floor committing a sexual act while watching her sleep. This is the kind of guy we were dealing with," Lewis said.

It was determined that Aunt Amy was aware of Leggs's status as a convicted sex offender, but he somehow convinced her that he wasn't a bad guy, enabling him to visit the house on a regular basis while developing a sordid "fancy" for Sarah and gaining the child's trust.

Records indicate that deputies quickly brought Leggs in for questioning. The suspect firmly denied any involvement in the disappearance of the child, claiming the younger sister was merely a troublemaker and that he had always avoided being alone with the girls because of his past. Everyone, Leggs said, got along very well.

"I knew within a few minutes that he had definitely committed the crime," Lewis recalled. "The way he snickered and smiled at my detectives, it was clear he thought he had committed the perfect crime. We had our man. We were just going have to prove it."

The felon pitched an alibi that he was at a bar with a friend the previous night although even his parents, with whom he resided, could not account for his whereabouts between 1 and 7 a.m., the timeframe Sarah went missing.

The investigation progressed when deputies discovered Sarah's toothbrush on the floorboard of Leggs's truck. Tires on the truck also matched marks in the snow outside the house where Sarah was abducted. While certainly not evidence of murder, his shed full of creepy pornographic videos and magazines only aggravated suspicions of perversion.

The largest search in the history of the community was generated. Thanks to cell phone records and pinging calls off three towers, deputies determined that Sarah was somewhere within a triangular portion of northern Wicomico County's outskirts.

Nearly three thousand residents volunteered to help, prompting Sheriff Lewis to establish a command post at the Delmarva Shorebirds baseball stadium. The endeavor needed to be organized so that well-intentioned people would not interfere with dive teams and boots-on-the-ground law enforcement concerned that a potential crime scene might be compromised.

Lewis said he "pleaded to everyone, once you go out and search your property, just tie a yellow ribbon around your mailbox, and when I went on another helicopter light after I did that, our whole community was littered with yellow ribbons everywhere."

Her body was found at a remote wooded spot within the geographical triangle near the Delaware border on Christmas Day. "I was like, 'thank god we found her,' but when I saw her and what he had done to her, and when I saw what was left of her, well, that was our Christmas. It was tough. It hurt us all, and I felt like we had failed," he lamented.

The victim had been sexually assaulted by Leggs, who choked and tried to drown her in a mud puddle. Apparently not satiated, he then departed the scene in his truck, bought gasoline, and returned to pour gasoline on Sarah, setting her ablaze. An autopsy concluded she was still alive when he burned her.

Leggs was arrested and charged for an unthinkably horrendous crime that shook Wicomico County to its foundation. "If ever there was a case that screamed for the death penalty, it was this case," the sheriff stated emphatically. "It was the brutal kidnapping, the brutal murder, and brutal destruction of this little girl's body that screamed for the death penalty. This man deserved to die."

The prosecutor, Abby Marsh, litigated the first sexual offense case in which Leggs was charged. People soon learned that he had been released from prison for "good behavior" just six months into his seven-year sentence.

Lewis said the State of Maryland sought the death penalty, but before the trial began, Leggs lodged a guilty plea in exchange for life in prison. Marsh reasoned that Leggs would never be free to hurt anyone again. Lewis said the predator bragged in the county lockup about his sexual assault of Sarah. Days after entering prison, he was slashed by a knife-wielding inmate in the dining hall without sustaining serious injuries.

In 2013 under Governor Martin O'Malley, Maryland became the eighteenth state in the union to abolish the death penalty.

The contempt for Leggs and the porous criminal justice system in social media threads was obvious:

> "R.I.P. Baby Girl. SO sorry this had to be you. May God Rest Your Soul. My Heart Hurts for you!"
>
> "I say let the S.O.B. be locked up in the regular prison and let the inmates kill him. This is a prime example of the flaws our criminal justice system contains."
>
> "My heart goes out to this poor child robbed of innocence then life."
>
> "This is such a tragedy. People need to be held responsible for putting their children in dangerous situations."
>
> "Something needs to be done about the justice system that allows monsters like this to walk among the innocent children of this

country."

"This is the failure of the parent/guardian to properly protect the child. This perp is a multi-level criminal and should NEVER have been on the street. His life should have been terminated at the time he was incarcerated for the rape of the sixteen-year-old."

"We desperately need "Risk Assessment" to better determine who is high risk and who isn't. The Tier system doesn't protect one soul. 93% of all new sex offenses are committed by people not on any registry."

scaredmonkeys.com

Lewis banned local blogger Joe Albero from his regular media contact list for falsely claiming Sarah's body had been found and that the sheriff's office was negligently withholding important details of the case.

"Everyone knows Albero wants to be the story rather than report it. I had gotten away from following his blog because it was divisive and how many people were saying he crossed the line. His blog is 100% proof you can lie and fabricate. He is a cancer to our society. I hope and pray he doesn't suffer a fatal injury in this county because the number of suspects would be extensive. If you don't like his lies and innuendo, don't look at the blog."

In January, only a month following Sarah's passing, Lewis received a standing ovation at the Maryland General Assembly when the Speaker of the House introduced him to testify on Sarah's behalf. While there was no reconciling the tragedy, Sarah Foxwell's death may have saved lives. Lewis and other advocates inspired "Sarah's Law" stipulating that convicted recidivistic sex offenders serve a minimum of fifteen years in prison without the possibility of parole.

Ricky Pollitt said Lewis's ability to kindly and professionally manage the Foxwell situation was a "defining moment for a very young sheriff."

"The way the sheriff handled the Foxwell case was a credit to him and crucial for the Wicomico County Sheriff's Office," seconded Lieutenant Robinson.

A replica grave marker, photo of the victim, commemorative coin, and a bag of rolled coins donated to the search for her by a tenyear-old boy are among the memorabilia displayed at the Wicomico County Sheriff's Office for Sarah Foxwell.

Every year, the community bonds around its recollection of Sarah Foxwell's demise. The following Christmas message from the sheriff's office in 2020 elicited numerous comments:

> "Please join the Wicomico County Sheriff's Office in remembering Sarah this Christmas. Delmarva's Christmas Angel will remain in the hearts of our deputies forever."
>
> "We all searched for that angel on that cold Christmas morning. My heart still hurts for her but swelled with pride seeing how hundreds of us forgot about opening our presents and came together to search for her. RIP Sweetie."
>
> "Sarah is never forgotten. Delmarva should always remember how everyone came together and remember what is really important in life. Bless you, Sarah."
>
> "Can't drive by the (Shorebirds) stadium in the season without thinking of the effort the community and sheriff's office put into trying to find her. Can't help but thinking of sheriff Lewis being so upset at the press conference. She won't be forgotten."
>
> *www.facebook.com/wicomicosheriff*

No one was murdered by the perpetrators of sex offenses at Mitchell's Martial Arts in Salisbury, but the painful case investigated by the Wicomico County Sheriff's Office drew significant publicity in 2016. Twenty-six-year-old karate instructor Zacharia Justice Bennett was sentenced to fifteen years in prison for victimizing three underaged girls at the school. His accomplice and fellow instructor, Leah Corrin Wright, twenty-one, received eighteen months behind bars for planning and participating in the atrocities.

The grandmother of one victim labeled Bennett as "cold and calculated" during his trial. One of the girls said she had befriended and trusted Wright, even thinking of her as a sister. Wright and the victim performed sex acts on Bennett together at the martial arts studio, according to testimony. Bennett also texted explicit pictures of himself to the young students.

Both convicted sexual predators will be considered "Tier 3 high risk" for the rest of their lives, prohibited from teaching, coaching, or volunteering around minors.

In 2018, Maryland became the seventeenth state in America to join the Offender Watch program that the Wicomico County Sheriff's Office had contracted with previously. There are nearly a million registered sexual offenders nationwide.

Lewis applauded the move to unify criminal justice resources against the scourge: "Wicomico County has been an Offender Watch client for several years. My agency saw the need very early on to adopt a program that not only allows the Sex Offender Registry to communicate with our neighboring counties and police departments but also can communicate in real-time with agencies of Maryland when potentially dangerous offenders move to Wicomico County. My citizens deserve the most accurate and timely notifications to protect their families. I am very happy that six million people will now have the ability to receive the same type of notification across Maryland."

While not considered a sex offense, sheer depravity afflicted the Wicomico County village of Eden in 2019, according to sheriff's office records. After beating up a man at a Sailfish Drive residence, Robert Glorious allegedly poured gasoline on the victim and set him afire. Deputies arrested Glorious and the driver of the getaway vehicle on Mount Hermon Road.

Glorious was charged with attempted first-degree murder, attempted second-degree murder, two counts of assault, reckless endangerment, violation of a governor's order, and arson. Deputies charged Emily Paige Skelton with being an accessory to the crime.

The severely burned victim was flown to Johns Hopkins Bayview Medical Center.

In the bin of barbarians, a man's arm was nearly amputated from the elbow down by assailants who tried to carve and burn off his tattoo at a house in Hebron. According to Sheriff Lewis, Paul Martin Hurst and Carey Lee Edwards were enraged that the victim had supposedly betrayed Juggalos, a fan base affiliated with the rap-metal duo Insane Clown Posse, considered a gang by the FBI. The suspects, both of whom were arrested by deputies, administered a severe beating prior to the atrocity.

It is sometimes impossible to understand what "triggers" human aggression, but sheriff's records indicate Jason Michael Layfield, a man with a criminal past, was drunk and irate over a pool game when he accosted occupants of a home off Parsonsburg Road. Deputies said Layfield threatened to take his own life, discharged a firearm outside the house, and shot a hole through the ceiling. He did not resist arrest.

Actual cold-blooded carnage in Wicomico County was committed by nineteen-year-old Myles David Lyons, who had the gall to argue with Judge Leah Jane Seaton when he was sentenced to three concurrent life sentences.

Records show he murdered Lakisha Jackson, thirty-nine, at a residence on Jersey Road by shooting her in the face with a shotgun and stabbing her in the chest. Jackson's teenaged daughter, Nicole, was eight months when he shot her in the chest and stabbed her in the face. He shot Tyisha Jackson, Nicole's sister, twice in the back.

Lyons fled the scene in a stolen car and was arrested a short time later by Dorchester County sheriff's deputies in Cambridge.

Parkside High School teacher Alice Davis, fifty-five, was reported missing by her husband. Authorities recovered her abandoned Honda automobile at the Wal mart in Fruitland. Investigators then discovered her body behind a church in Somerset County. She died from blunt trauma to the head. Her spouse, fifty-seven-year-old Jesse Davis, was linked to her murder and closely surveyed by deputies but committed suicide by slitting his wrists before he could be arrested, Lewis confirmed.

"Jesse Davis initiated a deliberate, calculated, and continuous course of deception and fabrications surrounding the disappearance of his wife," Lewis said. "Even when confronted with many inconsistencies and repeated lies, he continued to maintain, 'I don't know.'"

The victim was the sister of former Salisbury mayor Barrie Parsons Tilghman. The school held a vigil for Alice Davis in the auditorium. She loved teaching, Shakespeare, and cats.

Incredibly, in spite of the daunting necessity for accredited law enforcement officers to expunge pedophiles, murderers, serial killers, arsonists, gang bangers, the mentally demented, and other miscreants, disdain for policing has persisted.

Haven P. Simmons

CHAPTER FOUR

BALTIMORE BURNING AND THE NEFARIOUS
NARRATIVE

The breadth of responsibilities, outreach, reciprocated salutations, and pressure on sheriff's deputies and police officers to make split-second decisions aside, President Obama's second term featured extraordinary scrutiny of local law enforcement for myriad alleged monstrosities, pillorying and terminating cops defending themselves against savage assaults and worse, and commercial media ecstatically portraying every ugly encounter between a white officer and black civilian as racially motivated.

Unsurprisingly, Sheriff Lewis has noticed a decline in quality applicants for law enforcement positions. Any glamor or rush to wear the badge, pragmatic need for benefits and a solid salary, or genuinely altruistic motivations were compromised by the fear of failure, rebuke, and even arrest.

The Eastern Shore Criminal Justice Academy and its "highly skilled trainers" at Wor-Wic Community College in Salisbury is the primary vehicle for meeting the entry-level and in-service needs of the more than sixty agencies on the Maryland Eastern Shore.

"Applicants have dropped dramatically with the ongoing attacks on the law enforcement profession," Lewis said. "We wonder every day how to increase applicant pools."

As of 2020, starting yearly pay for a deputy was $45,430 with duties including all aspects of law enforcement activities entrusted to the Sheriff's Office of Wicomico County, Maryland. Requirements entailed certified Maryland police training, a physical agility test, polygraph, background investigation, mental and physical health examinations, computer competency, and a high school diploma or GED, according to the sheriff's office.

"When I came on the job in 1984, there was a great deal of respect and admiration for the very difficult task of being a police officer. Today, much of that respect, admiration, and public trust has eroded and not necessarily because of misconduct or corruption of police officers," said Lewis, going on to point out there are notable exceptions in every field.

By 2018, 40% of the nation's law enforcement officers had abandoned their jobs within five years. The Nashville Police Department, Seattle Police Department, and the FBI were among the agencies reporting a drastic reduction in applicants.

Maryland was recently the first state to repeal the law enforcement Bill of Rights, passing a package of reform measures diluting use of force, expanding the prevalence of body cameras, curbing departments from receiving surplus military equipment, limiting no-knock warrants, furthering public access to investigations of police misbehavior, and undercutting the ability of sheriffs and police chiefs to determine dismissal and disciplinary actions concerning officers.

Lewis said the legislation, which overrode a veto by Governor Larry Hogan, was devastating. "Policing as we've known it in Maryland is done. This is not law enforcement reform; it's law enforcement revenge."

The alterations were partially spurred by the demise of Anton Black in the small Eastern Shore town of Greensboro. Black died of cardiac arrest resisting police responding to a call that he was dragging a twelve-year-old boy down the street, later pinning the child against the hood of a patrol car. Officers resorted to tasing him.

Detractors of the legislation argued that it once again puts the onus on law enforcement for deeper social problems, deflating the recruitment and morale of officers. The emasculation of law enforcement and unrepentant virulence of cop haters poses a serious challenge:

"What do we want? Dead cops!" was chanted in New York.

"Pigs in a blanket; fry 'em like bacon," Saint Paul, Minnesota, Black Lives Matter marchers yelled.

"We're ready for what? We're ready for war!" bellowed protesters in Ferguson, Missouri.

Law Enforcement Today has received unspeakably disturbing anonymous messages about policing in recent years:

> "I hope you die, pigs. You are all racist bastards."
>
> "Police officers are an occupying force in America and need to be destroyed."
>
> "You'd better watch your back. Because we are watching it and when you aren't, you're going to find it pumped full of lead."
>
> "The only good cop is a dead cop. I hope your families all rot in hell."

Here are portions of a response from Kyle Reyes, the spokesman for the magazine:

> "Some people argue that we should ignore angry emails, messages, and letters that you send Law Enforcement Today. I can't. Because the hatred from those who hate the police is so misguided that I have to wonder where it came from. Robert (the owner of the publication, Robert Greenberg) is a cop. He has been for decades. He's accustomed to people swearing at police officers. Spitting at them. Threatening them. I'm not a cop. I've never been one. That's exactly WHY I was asked to be the National Spokesman for Law Enforcement Today.
>
> Because I can do things cops CAN'T do. I can run my mouth.
>
> I can take on trolls in ways they can't. I've seen the hostility. I've seen the attacks. And quite frankly, I'm sick of it. I was once part of it . . . sort of. I worked in the media for years. And during my time in the media, we were taught 'if it bleeds, it leads.' Perhaps the new saying should be 'if it makes cops look like pieces of shit, it leads.' Out-of-context body cam footage. Black Lives Matter rallies. Protests against police officers completely and legally justified in officer-involved shootings. (Cop haters) have to make decisions about what font type to use for protest signs. What street corner to stand on. What fake narrative you want to embrace in your antipolice tirade. But I want to ask a question to those of you who hate the police. Do you actually know why? I've been blessed to interview hundreds of cops in the last year alone.
>
> I've cried with the wives of officers killed in the line of duty. I've consoled fathers who have lost their kids who went into policing. I've had little children tell me about their dead dad who was a cop. This hatred has to stop."

Reyes signed his letter: Christian. Father. Husband. American.

The relevance of cohesive and empowered law enforcement in the incendiary narrative magnified tangibly on a national scale fairly early in Lewis's tenure, hastening his inclination to speak out.

A precursor to the massive riots was cast in 2012 as a racially motivated hate crime but did not actually involve a police officer. A seventeen-year-old black teenager named Trayvon Martin was fatally shot by neighborhood watch resident George Zimmerman during a physical confrontation in Florida, forever etching a bag of Skittles in the minds and palates of the general public.

In his book *Cop Under Fire*, African American Milwaukee County Sheriff David Clarke explained how desperately the media tried to portray Zimmerman as completely white rather than half-Hispanic, ostensibly doctoring his mug shot for viewing. "If you saw him in real life instead of on TV, you could see that his skin is brown. The media intentionally tried to make him look whiter because it's hard to sell a racial narrative without an evil white man attacking an innocent black man," said Clarke, who added that the photos aired of Martin were taken when he was five years younger and far less strapping.

The real catalyst behind bedlam in major cities, though, was the shooting in 2014 of eighteen-year-old Michael Brown, a black man, by a white police officer in Ferguson, Missouri, just outside Saint Louis. The death of another black man in New York, Eric Garner, incited further hatred for "racist" cops. Closer to home in Baltimore less than a year later, Freddie Gray, also black, died while being transported in a police van. In each instance, stories about what actually happened deviated strongly. Gray was a felon armed with a knife, and both Brown and Garner, harboring extensive criminal histories, resisted arrest.

A grand jury did not indict Officer Darren Wilson in the Michael Brown case, but he lost his job because the police department drew the wrath of too many citizens. The state's attorney said it was impossible to prove murder or manslaughter beyond a reasonable doubt.

Lewis criticized those who lambasted the decision, saying the officer acted appropriately. "Brown's behavior led to the outcome. He got what was coming to him that day. He wrote his own death ticket. He challenged that police officer, rushed him, he attempted to disarm him."

Friends reportedly paid for Wilson's legal fees. He has been unable to find work in law enforcement. Threats were made to harm his unborn child. He, his daughter, and two stepchildren reside at an undisclosed location. At one point, he was living in a home purchased by supporters near Saint Louis, with his name left off the deed for fear of retaliation.

The rallying cry "Hands Up, Don't Shoot!" proliferated from inaccurate assertions that Brown was trying to surrender. "I'm not going to keep living in the past about what Ferguson did. It's out of my control," Wilson said.

Lewis said, "At a decisive moment in our history when our nation requires strong and unbiased voices from its senior law enforcement officials, [Attorney General Eric Holder] has made it his personal mission to join other racial antagonists and politicize tragic events in this country," a dynamic provoked by the infamous "Ferguson effect."

None of the six officers charged in the death of Freddie Gray were actually convicted despite speculation about what caused his spinal cord injury during transport. The officer in the case of 350-pound Eric Garner, whose asthma conceivably contributed to his death, was terminated for applying a chokehold.

The alleged law enforcement war on black civilians instigated a war on cops. Over one August weekend in 2015, six police officers in Florida and Pennsylvania were gunned down mercilessly by assailants.

A black Maryland man made good on Facebook posts that he would drive to New York and execute two police officers in cold blood.

The targeted, premeditated violence diverged ominously from law enforcement fatalities that were historically more circumstantial (e.g., responding to a domestic disturbance, cornering an armed suspect, or making an unfortunate traffic stop).

A military veteran, who also happened to be black, massacred nine police officers and wounded five in Dallas in 2016 avenging what he perceived as unforgivable law enforcement indiscretions. According to the National Law Enforcement Memorial Fund, it was the deadliest day for the men and women in blue since 9/11.

Lewis was in an Ocean City restaurant celebrating the appointment of State's Attorney Maciarello to circuit judge when he learned what happened, quickly granting Fox News an interview about the tragedy.

"He loves his brothers and sisters of law enforcement. When we served, he was deeply wounded by what was happening (to police) nationally, regionally, and locally," Maciarello said. "How to deal with these issues seemed to be his greatest personal struggle."

"We have a segment of society that is very defiant. They hate law enforcement. And the Black Lives Matter movement perpetuated the violence," clarified Lewis, who was appalled by the Massachusetts police chief who shamelessly lay down on his stomach and pretended to be handcuffed by members of the group. "To be a strong leader, you can't bow down to political correctness. It upsets me when chiefs and sheriffs do not honor people who wear the badge."

"Sheriff Lewis is a role model for all counties in the state of Maryland. Honesty and strength," said Thomas Stitcher, a retired Salisbury University physical education professor and Air Force veteran. "In the climate today, law enforcement must be strong and relate to citizens. I want someone who will stand up to special interest groups."

The sheriff blamed President Barack Hussein Obama for fomenting racial unrest, enabling BLM, and refusing to genuinely denounce the attacks against cops. "It was his attitude toward law enforcement. He clearly did not like law enforcement."

It was "disgusting and despicable," Lewis said, that Obama spoke contentiously about the scenarios, precipitating chaos before all of the evidence was collected. Obama and his associates attended funerals for "thugs" who assaulted police, he added, but not those remembering police officers killed in the line of duty.

"Black LIES Matter is not your grandfather's civil rights movement. It's the illegitimate child of these debunked racial incidents and the spawn of radical leftist activists," Clarke said. "The founders of the movement have more in common with David Duke than Martin Luther King, Jr."

Clarke considers the three founders of the group leeches who "took advantage of racial strife" to enter the national stage. "They're radical activists who hold values that most Americans don't share—

that most black Americans don't share. It should come as no surprise to you that they are opposed to the nuclear family. Instead, they propose a black 'village.' Only 'mothers' and 'parents' exist in their fantasy," apparently oblivious to the undermining dearth of patriarchy in many urban communities.

The four-term Milwaukee sheriff then upped the ante: "When (white liberals) proudly stand up and demand that marriage comes in many different flavors—or, more accurately, that it doesn't matter at all— they're promoting an idea that creates higher risks for poverty, lower educational attainment, and family instability. They are actually hurting poor people, not themselves."

Years earlier, according to Lewis, Governor Martin O'Malley set a bad and cowardly precedent when he apologized for saying "all lives matter" rather than only "black lives matter."

"Of course, all lives matter," railed the sheriff. "Why did he apologize? Because he quickly found it was politically incorrect. That's what makes me sick to my stomach. Political correctness is destroying this country. We need to take this country back."

Lewis's candor infuriated Barbara Waters of nearby Snow Hill in Worcester County: "I would like to hear a good reason why Wicomico County still has a man on the payroll with the reasoning of Mike Lewis. He is a good reason not to pay taxes if that means he gets paid. Black Lives Matter, and so do white ones, because we are all equal. How can he make so many redneck remarks publicly every time something happens, and still be a servant to all people? He can start a lot of trouble with his mouth. I am so glad all of Wicomico County does not think like him."

Mardela Springs resident Tom Mooney succinctly refuted Waters and people of similar persuasion:

> "Recently, two of Wicomico County's liberal Democrats spoke about Sheriff Mike Lewis' comments as to who is to blame for recent attacks on law enforcement officers. They always seem to bash Republicans. Geoff Smoot in his letter claims the County Council should censure the sheriff. I believe this great nation gave us unalienable rights, one of which was freedom of speech. I am sure that he as a retired history teacher, Smoot taught—or should have taught—many of the rights we enjoy. Mike Pretl goes on in his letter about how much money has come from President Obama for (law enforcement) training and equipment. He seems to forget about Congress. Seized money from the sale of vehicles impounded by law enforcement goes back to the department that seized it. If there is an incident like those that have happened in other areas, our sheriff and his deputies will step forward. I have every confidence that Lewis will resolve it without the use of force."

The residue of discord eventually manifested at a home on Rockawalkin Road. The sheriff and several deputies responded to a call from a man claiming he had shot a family member and intended to shoot others. Lewis termed it a "spoofing incident" when a search of the house revealed no evidence supporting the story. Investigators learned the complainant was seeking attention after identifying him on Facebook stomping one American flag and burning a second to protest against the country and the police.

Lewis said the idea that black civilians were being singled out egregiously by white police officers on the basis of race has been debunked. Minorities comprise a significant percentage of police officers making arrests in densely populated, high-crime metropolitan areas rife with blight, drugs, gangs, and weapons.

Not only that, the thought of an imminent race war was confounded by the reality that most crime is white-on-white, black-on-black, Hispanic-on-Hispanic, Asian-on-Asian, and Native American-on Native American. Blacks were murdered overwhelming by other blacks in crime-ridden cities across America, dispelling accusations that racist police perpetrated most of the killings.

"If we racialize the discussion of crime and punishment and policing in America, we are playing with fire," said Dr. Glenn Loury, the first tenured African American economics professor at Harvard University. Loury pointed out that more white people are killed by police each year and that media "organs" MSNBC, CNN, CBS News, and the *New York Times* avoid conceding the astronomical black crime rates in major cities that deter people from leaving their homes.

"I don't see 'systemic' racism in Wicomico County," Lewis said. "I don't see it in the men and women of the Wicomico County Sheriff's Office patrolling our streets."

According to author Heather Mac Donald, "the anti-cop movement and its high-placed political and media enablers remained impervious to all facts contradicting their 'policing is racist' narrative. They were also indifferent to the mounting loss of black lives. Officers in minority neighborhoods were backing off proactive policing, under the constant refrain that such policing was racist. As a consequence, violence accelerated."

"There is an increased potential for officers being criminally liable for making a good faith mistake," lamented Hampton, Virginia, Police Chief Terry Sult.

The owners of Ben & Jerry's ice cream, founded in a left-leaning Vermont haven near the home of presidential hopeful Bernie Sanders, have begun lobbying for legislation to eliminate law enforcement officer immunity from lawsuits tapping their personal bank accounts and real estate possessions.

Social justice warrior Shaun King and rapper Michael "Killer Mike" Render endorsed the business owners, who petitioned to hold a new trial for Mumia Abu-Jamal, convicted of murdering a police officer.

Resentment quickly emanated from law enforcement proponents:

> "Hope BLM responds to your calls for service."
>
> "These two liberal, cop-hating scumbags don't deserve any business from anyone who values cops and the dangers they face."
>
> "All police officers and family members should boycott these Communists who attempted to free a cop killer in Philadelphia. Maybe we should just defund all police departments and see how people like this would fare on their own . . . would be a very interesting situation."
>
> "I can still never get used to the staggering hypocrisy that is the left. They say all cops are racists. They say all cops should be subject to being sued for doing their jobs. They say all cops are bad based on stories spoon-fed to them by a hostile news media before any investigation has been done. But you go and say all members of a certain race or group or political party are all bad, when you're not a member of the far left, and watch what happens to you."
>
> *Police Law Enforcement Solutions website*

Fairly early in Lewis's tenure as sheriff, Vernon J. Leftridge sued three deputies, including Sergeant Michael Kelly Matthews, for alleged racism during an early morning traffic stop on US 13. Deputies purportedly pulled him over because a brake light on his car was out

Based on possessing no registration, having a different last name than his brother who was a passenger, conflicting stories about where they were traveling, and apparent nervousness, the two men were patted down, and a K-9 search of the vehicle was conducted.

Only remnants of marijuana leaves were located. Sergeant Matthews issued Leftridge a warning, shook hands with both men, and according to video and audio documentation, wished them a safe trip. Video also refuted claims that Leftridge and his brother were subjected to overzealous, invasive strip searches.

The lawsuit faltered when the judge declared, "There is no evidence that any deputy, in this case, said or did anything during the encounter that would give any outward appearance of racial bias or ulterior motive for their actions. There are no unexplained discrepancies in the deputies' conduct, nor did the deputies make seemingly off topic comments with racial overtones. I recognize that Mr. Leftridge suspected a racial motive for the stop. But a lawsuit must be built on facts, not suspicion."

Beyond the outcome of the litigation and implicit faith in his deputies, Lewis maintains that "racism and discrimination are inexcusable. There is no place for this type of behavior—and that certainly includes the Wicomico County Sheriff's Office. We will not tolerate these actions in our community. Our core values state and reflect that our deputies will treat every person with respect and dignity, and in an unbiased manner, and protect the constitutional rights of all persons through impartial enforcement of the law. I have enforced that premise since my first day in office."

Meanwhile, people increasingly wondered whether anarchy wrapped in the cloak of "social justice" was possible in the United States. Theories about federalizing the police intensified. The men and women in blue were sullied for being the "enforcement" component of government.

"The campaign against cops is a battle in a larger culture war, in which one camp seeks to redefine the American experience as the continual oppression of an ever-growing number of victim groups," Mac Donald said. "Social norms, the legitimacy of authority, the rule of law—all are denigrated as the machinery of oppression, and the police are tarred as the most conspicuous embodiment of injustice."

David M. Watson of Laurel, Delaware, and Delmar, Maryland, resident Orrin Joudray, who took a plea deal, were sentenced to 106 and 15 years, respectively, for shooting rifles and shotguns at the homes of law enforcement officers in Sussex County, Delaware, and Wicomico County.

"I come from a very long line of civil service. I never, ever expected to be putting my family in danger," said Dewey Beach Police Department Sergeant Clifford Dempsey, one of the victims. "I will forgive you someday. I can't say the same for my children."

Delaware Superior Court Judge T. Henley Graves said he was dispensing a sentence to ensure Watson dies in prison.

Following his arrest, Watson escaped two Wicomico County Detention Center officers who were transporting him to Clifton T. Perkins Psychiatric Hospital in Jessup, Maryland. Watson was found by Howard County police hiding in a drain pipe, having eluded capture for six days. He stole a hard hat and work vest to distract law enforcement search teams, eating out of trash cans and drinking water from puddles to survive.

In April 2021, a Wicomico County sheriff's deputy and a state trooper discovered savagely beaten Corporal Keith Heacock of the Delmar, Delaware, Police Department only minutes from Salisbury. Heacock had initially responded to a residence alone after the alleged assailant, thirty-year-old Randon Wilkerson, also brutally attacked an elderly couple, breaking both of the woman's eye sockets. The twenty-two-year law enforcement veteran died from brain injuries several days later in a Baltimore hospital.

The dastardly, brazen assaults are not confined to police. Firefighters, paramedics, and EMTs (Emergency Medical Technicians) have begun wearing bulletproof vests to protect themselves against assailants. First responders, fearing harassment and atrocities, are sometimes obliged to wait in staging areas until law enforcement secures the scene for adequate emergency response. Disruptive bystanders, some of them armed, scream obscenities and record responders' every move on cell phones.

Reports show that Leron Devin Mitchell, thirty-one, was recently arrested for assaulting a paramedic providing medical care for his brother at a residence on Old Ocean City Road. The agitated Mitchell kept yelling at responders from the Parsonsburg Volunteer Fire Company when they arrived. He jumped into the back of the ambulance as paramedics were gathering their equipment, striking one of them in the head for not moving fast enough.

His head bleeding, the volunteer used his body to block the door of the bedroom in the house so that he could assist the brother without further interference. Mitchell fled before Wicomico County sheriff's deputies appeared but, because of multiple warrants, was arrested by the capital fugitives task force.

Mitchell was charged with second-degree assault on EMS, obstructing and hindering, and making a false statement to an officer.

The obsession with "handcuffing" police, most recently manipulated as "defunding" or "reimagining" law enforcement, has jeopardized law-abiding citizens with crime rates blasting through the stratosphere in large cities such as Chicago, Saint Louis, and Baltimore, a location Sheriff Lewis and his deputies became quite familiar with.

"Baltimore Burning" referred to massive riots in 2015. Media images depicted a veritable inferno with fires and plumes of smoke spreading across the night sky, indelibly etching the worst possible impressions of "Charm City" in the American psyche. The carnage badly exacerbated the tendency of people to only associate Baltimore with the state of Maryland rather than the mountainous panhandle, the Eastern Shore, or other cities skirting the nation's capital. Sections of the city were a charred wasteland when the fires subsided. The almost incalculable damage included locally-owned private businesses that took years to build. Decent, law-abiding residents ran for their lives when the peaceful protest was hijacked by bands of thugs and scavengers.

For years, the fulcrum of lawlessness in Baltimore has not only been organized gangs but teenage "flash mobs" hastily formed through social media messaging. When they heard of a free Slurpees giveaway at a 7-Eleven, for instance, a mob crammed the store, stole

$6,000 worth of merchandise, and severely beat the manager who attempted to intercede. One Saint Patrick's Day, a youth was stabbed and a tourist pummeled, robbed, and stripped of his clothes as other people amongst the city's supposedly proudest destination, the Inner Harbor, sought refuge from marauding predators in a nearby hotel. Teenagers also euphorically play a "knockout" game where unsuspecting bystanders are sucker-punched in the head.

Sheriff Lewis was receiving the "Person of the Year" award on a Saturday night at the Elks Club when he was notified by one of his deputies that riots, inflamed by fliers and social media at the Baltimore Mall, were breaking out in the city. He texted Baltimore police commissioner Anthony Batts, offering to assist with Wicomico County Sheriff's Office assets.

By Monday, anticipating the worst upheaval following Freddie Gray's funeral, officials accepted help from WCSO, as Lewis, a dozen deputies including the SWAT team, and the Wicomico County Sheriff's Office MRAP vehicle converged with six hundred law enforcement officers from around the state of Maryland and elsewhere at ground zero.

"The cops are getting their asses handed to them. If anyone throws a solo cup at you, arrest them," Lewis implored his deputies as they prepared for their journey to the Western Shore. "We need to get them off the street."

Upon arrival in Baltimore for their primary assignment to guard the police department and city hall, Wicomico sheriff's deputies observed a Baltimore Police Department vehicle that had been torched. Hooligans perched on roofs of police cars, breaking out their windshields. Rioters used garbage cans as projectiles. Many onlookers and participants gleefully recorded the violence on their cell phones while television cameras rolled. Too frequently, rioters were cheered and police officers jeered by the crowds.

Downtown, he said, emitted a "putrid smell" of scorched tires and incessant, deafening noise from the upheaval. "I counted eleven helicopters from the National Guard and TV stations circling overhead."

According to Lewis, "[The MRAP] was actually used to transport sheriff's deputies and other law enforcement personnel from one location to the next in the city. The Baltimore Police Department was well aware of the reasons I was bringing it to the city, and they determined they wanted my MRAP because it was the largest militarized armored vehicle present during the entire riots. The vehicle was also positioned at strategic points on different days to protect churches, businesses, and city hall. We were met by three thousand to five thousand demonstrators and violent protesters who were looting, rioting, and burning vehicles on the street."

Any hopes of making a palpable difference in the enforcement realm, however, were quickly dashed.

"[Law enforcement] was told by the mayor (Stephanie Rawlings Blake) to stand down," Lewis said disbelievingly. "It was unlike anything I had experienced in law enforcement. I couldn't understand for the life of me what was going on." There was no apparent pushback from the police commissioner.

While cordoning off the three-block radius around the police department and city hall, Lewis said, his deputies witnessed felonious assaults, looting, and burning, with little recourse as the mayhem imperiled businesses and citizens, some of whom were terrified motorists.

People inside a nearby church and on the street flipped off the deputies and first responders, "mouthing vulgar obscenities." Over their fourteen hours with scant relief, exhausted Wicomico deputies endured tear gas as rampaging rioters attempted to overwhelm the area, according to Lewis. It was total chaos perpetrated by "thugs taking over the city with complete impunity."

Baltimore police navigating the police department barricades set up by his deputies were mortified by the "stand down and retreat" edicts. "I was talking to a number of senior commanding officers who were delegated authority throughout the city, and there were dozens of officers coming and going," Lewis recounted. "They were clearly worn out. They were embarrassed, apologizing that we had to come to Baltimore city. They were saying they were done—that they were through—and the mayor allowed them to get pelted."

He continued, "My officers and I stared at each other in disbelief that these men and women were sent into harm's way and told to stand down. I heard that on the Baltimore city police radio for two days, and these guys were going through hell. We saw carloads of four to six BPD officers retreating. They were being outflanked by rioters with bricks, bottles, and Molotov cocktails. I was up there in armored gear because I was ready to do battle."

One hundred and seventy Baltimore police officers were injured in the rioting, forty-three seriously, something that was not publicized enough according to the sheriff. "Some could not come back to work.

Their careers were over."

Previewing a pattern five years later across the country, the rioters were almost one hundred percent black early on, said Lewis, but encroaching whites proved to be belligerent, obnoxious antagonists.

"The days that followed were white people coming in by carloads to demonstrate and protest, most of which had gauges (a form of body piercing where the ear's skin is stretched) and were covered in tattoos," Lewis said. "Their hands were constantly waving in the air with their fingers up in my face, inches from my face, while videotaping with their cell phones."

Surreal developments emerged at city hall when the mayor and her staff were negotiating a truce with the Bloods, Crips, and other gangs that threatened to abandon their turf battles for a unified attack against law enforcement. "We were told not to search (gang members) when they came to city hall," Lewis said.

Lewis was gratified, though, when local restaurant owners donated food to police and first responders. He personally handed out fruit and bottled water to National Guard members and fellow law enforcement officers who eventually relieved his deputies.

"We had residents thanking us for being there. They were grateful for our help," Lewis said. Neill Franklin, a leader in the African American community and marijuana advocate, burst into tears and hugged the sheriff at city hall, indicative of the trauma felt by many residents.

The Freddie Gray episode emboldened opportunists and edgy residents in Baltimore expecting the worst from law enforcement.

"Meech" Tucker, a convicted felon, was running from police when his gun discharged. Tucker dropped to the ground, pretending to have been shot by the officers. Witnesses and toughs flung bricks, water, and Clorox bottles at the police vindictively as rumors miscasting the scenario immersed the community.

Looting, fires, and vandalization destroyed 350 businesses in Baltimore. Sheriff Lewis was later deposed to testify by attorneys representing business owners who sued the City of Baltimore for failing to defend them during the chaos.

Fox News reporter Leland Vittert approached the sheriff with a caveat. "He said he knew I could not give him an interview as a law enforcement official because the mayor said, so I told him that I work for the people of Wicomico County, not the mayor of Baltimore, and gave him the interview," said Lewis, holding true to his propensity for addressing the media bluntly and punctually.

By the time Lewis and his deputies departed Baltimore, he had spoken to the Middle East network Al-Jazeera, the British Broadcasting Corporation (BBC), FOX, and CNN, never shy about his frustration with groveling Baltimore officials who catered to the rioters.

"Baltimore Burning" elevated Sheriff Lewis's profile from Wicomico County, the Eastern Shore, the state of Maryland, and the region, to national and global heights. He spoke with the late radio icon Rush Limbaugh and was interviewed on several occasions by Sean Hannity. The conference room of the sheriff's office began to feel like a television studio.

"They're (law enforcement) very fearful to go out there and be proactive—which we all should be doing in law enforcement today," Lewis told Hannity. "Especially in urban areas. The officers are no longer proactive and as you can see, the violence has surged."

A "Mike Lewis for President" social media site emerged. "He tells it like it is. I totally commend him for the job he is doing," said a former Ocean City police and Eastern Correctional Institution (ECI) officer, praising his refusal to "sugar coat" or "hide" from the dreadful realities.

He and the Wicomico County Sheriff's Office encountered choppy waters with Salisbury's Gannett daily newspaper as the tumult boiled over. The *Daily Times* printed a cartoon depicting brutal, flak jacketed police tasing a black man and holding reporters at bay with a firearm, something Lieutenant Robinson did not see the humor in when he posted a photo on his personal Facebook page of a *Daily Times* delivery tube in a trash receptacle.

Robinson's supposed insolence infuriated Executive Editor Michael Kilian, who messaged Sheriff Lewis directly while copying Robinson and several county officials: "I realize some people in local law enforcement did not like the cartoon we published Wednesday regarding local police in the Ferguson, MO situation. But for a public official, particularly one who is a liaison with the news media, to post a disparaging photo of a newspaper is infantile. Lt. Robinson's actions make *The Daily Times* seriously concerned about his ability to be fair and whether he is your best person available to us and by extension the public."

Lewis's ambition to stand his ground righteously was solidified by the attack on Lieutenant Robinson. He said the cartoon did not mention Ferguson specifically, degrading law enforcement agencies everywhere, including Wicomico County. In his mind, it further demeaned local deputies and police officers who had recently been accosted, assaulted, and fired upon in the line of duty.

Here are excerpts from his response to the editor:

"After you made the incendiary decision to publish the shocking and disparaging cartoon generally depicting all law enforcement as a bunch of racist, gun-toting goons, who routinely hold the press hostage while failing to release pertinent information, I'm shocked that you have the audacity to personally email me to 'express' your dismay at the unprofessionalism of Lt. Robinson of the Wicomico County Sheriff's Office. (Lt. Robinson) is a very educated, hardworking, loyal member of this agency and our community. We have bent over backward to work with and accommodate the paper on many stories of public interest. We've always treasured our local *Daily Times* and the relationship we have shared, as it serves to inform our community on issues of public safety, while showcasing the dedicated work being performed by the talented men and women of the Wicomico County Sheriff's Office. Your latest publication was meant to fuel the anger that churns beneath the surface of many Americans, both black and white. Your 'infantile' decision to publish this garbage has left an indelible mark on the many law enforcement professionals who leave their families to protect yours."

Citing Ferguson and Baltimore as catalysts, an Austin, Texas, police officer alluded to diminishing media and public perceptions of law enforcement: "All of a sudden, I read the news and got a strong feeling that certain parts of our society felt that I was a jack-booted thug who evil-laughed while finding ways to violate people's civil rights. That's a tough pill to swallow for someone who took the job to be one of the good guys."

"You get burned by suspects. You get burned by the people you are trying to help. You get burned by the criminal justice system. You get burned by the DA's office and the City Council," the disgruntled officer told *Law Enforcement Today* after resigning prematurely.

Houston Police Chief Art Acevedo excoriated liberal politicians in Austin for the poor showing of Democrats in statewide elections: "Texas Democrats can blame socialist democrats and the defund the police crowd led by Greg Casar, Jimmy Flannigan and the rest of the Austin City Council. Fact, Americans and Texans want better policing, not de-policing, and they won't want anything to do with any form of socialism."

"Being a police officer is only easy in a police state," mused a veteran Florida cop, inviting comparisons to China, Russia, the Philippines, and other foreign countries with muzzled media and a paucity of tolerance for social unrest.

Two months after assuming office, President Biden inked an executive order to increase voting and voter registration among criminals on probation and in prison, compelling the attorney general and US Marshals office to furnish advice regarding how to proceed.

The treachery of commercial and social media in America was profound preceding, during, and after the election of Donald Trump, a staunch supporter of law enforcement. Lewis is no stranger to belligerent national media, saying he was labeled a "bull-necked, megaphone, caffeinated drug warrior" by a *New York Times Magazine* reporter during his years as a state trooper.

Trump's media savvy contributed significantly to his victory, later castigating "fake news" and a media obsession to topple him. He reveled in flummoxing the politicos, pundits, and pollsters with seemingly utter revulsion for the political correctness paralyzing the nation.

Lewis met Trump in 2016 when he was campaigning on the Eastern Shore. The arrival of Trump's personal plane, the largest ever to land at the Salisbury Regional Airport, caused quite a buzz around the region. Sheriff Lewis was the first to greet the billionaire as he de-planed: "Welcome to the Eastern Shore, sir. You are in Trump country."

A high-security escort ensued to Stephen Decatur High School in Berlin, the site of Trump's rally. Lewis said he was notified of the visit only two days in advance. The Secret Service vetted deputies and briefed the sheriff's office on the arrangements. The Wicomico County Sheriff's Office, Worcester County Sheriff's Office, and the Maryland State Police collaborated with federal agents to ensure the Republican candidate's safety.

Lewis keeps a glossy photo album of the special occasion and the seven White House visits in his office.

Twenty-four deputies and Sheriff Lewis also joined the huge security detail for Trump's inauguration. "It's an honor to be part of this transition of power. You don't see this in all the other countries around the world. It's on honor that the men and women of the Wicomico County Sheriff's Office were asked to do this. It is something they can be proud of the rest of their lives," Lewis enthused.

While his deputies made no arrests, Lewis said they were prepared to. "We went over with some trepidation, knowing certain people wanted to disrupt the process. We had heard they might be throwing urine and feces-filled balloons at cops. We would have held them accountable."

Career politicians in the cozy, unwelcoming two-party system inside the beltway labeled "the swamp" by Trump found the "outsider" farcical and offensive—a comb-over caricature, reality TV star, and self-puffing buffoon. Television talking heads and editorial writers from major newspapers said he would never win.

But Trump's entertainment value was alluring, boosting ratings at left-leaning networks like CNN and MSNBC that unwittingly strengthened his prospects. The billionaire's availability for interviews without a horde of staffers to run interference, willingness to hold frequent press conferences, and the sheer power of his personality negated the narrative.

For better or worse, depending upon political preferences, "The Donald's" brashness influenced the future of the social media sphere as he eagerly tweeted his base, sometimes in the middle of the night.

Trump pinned derogatory nicknames on Republicans such as Marco Rubio, Ted Cruz, and Jeb Bush, the equivalent of political royalty, prior to vanquishing "Crooked Hillary" in the general election. His bravado alienated some Americans and tantalized others that were tired of measuring their opinions in politically-correct quicksand.

Lewis grew to respect Trump immensely, but his first choice was Rubio after meeting him during a clandestine operation with the

Columbian police to assess the region's drug trafficking ventures. "He translated Spanish for us," Lewis said. "I liked his enthusiasm for what we were doing, and I liked his domestic policies. I offered to help his ground game in Maryland."

Although accepting the use of non-euphoric medical marijuana, Rubio shares Lewis's opposition to decriminalizing illegal drugs and the legalization of cannabis.

In addition to pollster predictions echoed loudly by the media weeks and months before the actual vote, most of the "experts" failed to detect a segment of America lionizing Trump in rural areas, small towns, and "flyover" states that felt disenfranchised, largely omitted from the national dialogue. Their rallies should have been warning enough for his reptilian detractors in the swamp who consumed "humble pie" at Thanksgiving dinner as the eight-thousand-pound hippo waded in on their territory.

According to *The Case for Trump* author Victor David Hanson, however, the interloper would soon encounter "a brave new world of telecommunications, computers, the Internet, and social media without guidance from the past about whether these international and global megacompanies qualified as public utilities, monopolies, or trusts. As progressive, quasi-independent, and autonomous states, they made their own laws. Silicon Valley and its affiliates hardly feared what they felt was the passing irritant of a Trump presidency despite their zealous efforts to have prevented it and now to derail it."

Lewis joined forty-three other top law enforcement officials in the Green Room of the White House when President Trump unleashed an invective at media plainly desiring his ouster. According to the sheriff, Trump shamed them for being phony, disgraceful, and dishonest while recalling a malicious piece in the *New York Times*.

"He made me very proud of how he handled himself. I thought he was in control. As you could see, he turned and directed his comments many times to the sheriffs. We reassured him, 'We've got your back, Mr. President, because you always have ours.'"

Lewis, who was among those clapping when the president made his remarks, said people texted photos of him looking pleasantly surprised. "We were all thrilled to have a front-row seat to what occurred in that room."

"We never had a president like Trump who expressed his gratitude to law enforcement and first responders. More police officers were being stalked, attacked, and killed when Obama was president. The bad guys were emboldened by him," Sheriff Lewis said.

Nearly every law enforcement organization in America endorsed Trump's quest for re-election, among them the Wicomico County Fraternal Order of Police Lodge 111 comprised of local agencies and the state police.

"We Back the Blue. It is time to stand up to DEFEND law enforcement, not to defund it," attested the United States Deputy Sheriff's Association, which has focused on training and equipment upgrades for local agencies since its inception over twenty-five years ago.

USDSA training and program director Mike Willis welcomed 2021 by saying the preceding year was "especially difficult for the men and women of law enforcement due to a false narrative about law enforcement and the unrest that ensued in many locations. The overwhelming majority are professionals who serve not for fame, and certainly not for fortune, but with passion and a sense of duty to their community."

As the infernal racial discontent reminiscent of five years earlier was spread by Antifa, Black Lives Matter, acquiescing politicians, faculty and administrators in higher education, and other elements, the difference between peaceful protests and rioting was painfully evident to rational Americans. Sheriff Lewis publicly praised the comportment of Wicomico County residents in a statement inspired by his agency's "core values" of courage, honor, and integrity:

"Wicomico County has been the site of peaceful assemblies and rallies. I thank members of our community for expressing their thoughts and emotions in a positive and productive way while not losing sight of the tragic death of George Floyd. Citizens should never be without a voice, and the men and women of the Wicomico County Sheriff's Office and I will always be ready to defend your Constitutional rights, without fear of violence. Like any person with a heart who watched the video released in the death of George Floyd, I was shocked, angered, frustrated, and deeply concerned by what I saw. Watching a person lose his life is heartbreaking and emotional. As an elected sheriff who believes in law and order, I believe people who commit violent crimes should be prosecuted to the fullest extent of the law, and face stiff penalties. At this point of the ongoing investigation, the officers in the video have been formally charged and evidence is being collected and analyzed, and statements are being obtained and evaluated in the pursuit of justice. The attorney general of Minnesota is investigating the case and the process could take months. At the Wicomico County Sheriff's Office, we continue to re-evaluate police tactics and techniques while ensuring that nationally recognized best practices are integrated into our twenty-first-century policing. The Wicomico County Sheriff's Office was one of the first in this entire region to equip patrol deputies with both in-car cameras and body-worn cameras to ensure the highest levels of transparency. You deserve nothing less. We strive to harness the power of every individual through education, training, and volunteerism to make Wicomico

> County safer, stronger, and better prepared to respond to civil
> disturbances of any kind. The levels of training, communication,
> cooperation, and professionalism in our county's law enforcement
> arena have never been higher or more inclusive. It is up to all of us to
> leave this world a better place than it is today, and I believe the
> conversations occurring as a result of Mr. Floyd's tragic death will
> drive that conversation."

While delivering assurances and fostering dialogue in the community, Lewis said he told members of an African American ministerial group and other parties that those disrupting peaceful protests with "destruction and violence" in Wicomico County "will see a side of me they wish they had never seen."

Floyd's demise was indeed the catalyst behind nationwide protests that frequently devolved into looting, burning, destruction, and violence. The video showed white Minneapolis police officer Derek Chauvin kneeling on the neck of Floyd for nine minutes as he was handcuffed face-down on the street. Floyd, who had been convicted of assault and robbery, theft, firearm, and narcotics violations in the past, was being arrested for supposedly trying to pass a bogus $20 bill at a nearby store.

The rioting in Minneapolis mesmerized Americans, who watched portions of the city literally burn to the ground. Marylanders could certainly relate, having witnessed comparable destruction in Baltimore five years prior.

Bob Kroll, head of the union representing Minneapolis police, said the event ignited a "terrorist movement" that had been building and festering for years. He added that some city leaders "have been minimizing the size of our police force and diverting funds to community activists with an anti-police agenda. Our chief requested four hundred more officers and was flatly denied any. That is what led to this record-breaking riot."

Entertainers and athletes condemning the death aligned with social justice warriors around the country. Football and basketball players continued the tradition from 2015 of kneeling before games. Buffalo Bills players remained in the locker room as the national anthem was played before the AFC 2021 championship game, only days after professional basketball star Kyrie Irving purchased a home for Floyd's family. Dallas Mavericks owner Mark Cuban refused to play the national anthem at home games until the NBA interceded.

In the interim, Sheriff Lewis said he received backlash for urging protesters at the Baltimore Ravens' M&T Bank Stadium to concentrate on being productive citizens.

Many celebrities complained of "systemic racism," promoted defunding police, and opened their wallets from opulent, gated homes removed from the mayhem. Chrissy Teigen donated $100,000 to bail rioters out of jail. Kyle Jenner, through her corporation Kyle Cosmetics, gave to Black Lives Matter, Campaign Zero, the Equal Justice Initiative, Youth Justice Coalition, and the NAACP. The civil rights advocacy group Color of Change received money from Justin Bieber's clothing brand. Ellen DeGeneres was generous to Black Lives Matter and the ACLU, among others. Angelina Jolie augmented the NAACP Legal Defense Fund.

Contrition was a constant theme in their public commentary. "I do things every day without fear, because I am privileged, and I am privileged every day because I am white," posted former One

Direction band member Harry Styles with a blaring Black Lives Matter backdrop. "Being not racist is not enough, we must be antiracist. I stand in solidarity with all of the protesters."

Zuby, the British rapper and podcaster, said it is customary for naive celebrities to adopt the liberal narrative: "If you defund the police or you abolish the police, who is it going to hurt? It's not going to be the celebrities who have private security and live in gated communities. It's easy for them to be anti-border walls and anti-guns when they are surrounded by border walls and guns," as opposed to fearful residents of areas teeming with crime.

George Floyd Square was established in Minneapolis, a spontaneous memorial with street art, paintings, flowers, assorted gifts, and protest signs claiming the city was over-policing.

Following Floyd's passing, caustic demonstrations erupted in many Democrat-run cities across America, raising other alleged instances of police misconduct.

"I will hold the line until the very end. I believe in law and order," said Lewis, who attributed the non-violent protests in Wicomico County to "the relationships we have worked so hard to build over the years."

Presumptive vice-presidential nominee Kamala Harris revered the upheaval, bragging there was more to come. Riots also occurred in Philadelphia, New York, and Atlanta, where the CNN building sustained damage. In Washington, D.C., the security perimeter at the White House was nearly breached as the president and first lady sequestered inside.

New York police officers "have reached the breaking point over the past two weeks," said Patrick Lynch, president of the Police Benevolent Association. "We have been attacked in the streets, demonized in the media, and denigrated by every politician in this city."

"This is what the politicians wanted—no bail, nobody in Rikers prison, cops not arresting anyone," said an NYPD officer as the number of robberies, shootings, and homicides soared.

New York Mayor Bill de Blasio's history of pouring gasoline on the racial fire is reprehensible. He says that he agonizes about his biracial son potentially being brutalized by "officers paid to protect him." New York police were irate, circulating a form requesting that de Blasio not attend their funerals should they be killed in the line of duty.

Approximately seventy percent of Washington, D.C., cops contemplated quitting because of the unabridged violence. Among other provisions, the city passed an emergency reform bill expanding training requirements and publicly naming officers involved in shootings before their cases were reviewed.

Two Louisville police officers were shot during riots in the aftermath of Breonna Taylor's death. A news crew for the NBC television network was among those attacked, and law enforcement made 127 arrests.

Plain clothes Louisville undercover narcotics squad members, who were not equipped with body cameras to document exactly what occurred, executed a search warrant of her home that had supposedly been used as a base of illicit operations for Jamarcus Glover,

Breonna's former boyfriend and a reputed drug dealer.

Police said they announced their intention to enter the residence even though it was a "no-knock" warrant. When no one answered, according to officers, they used a battering ram to open the door.

A visitor at the residence, Kenneth Walker, said he fired his gun at them thinking there was an illegal break-in occurring. Officers returned fire, reports said, killing Taylor. Walker was not wounded.

"Defund the police" went a step further in Louisville with the "Abolish the police" refrain advanced by protesters.

"I am repulsed by the notion that anyone would want to defund the police," huffed Lewis, repeating that murder and crime rates in countless American cities have risen exponentially.

The Louisville backlash, fueled by Black Lives Matter proponents, ramped up when a grand jury declined to charge two of the three officers in the case. Officer Brett Hankinson, who had been terminated by the department, was charged with wanton endangerment.

"My role, as special prosecutor in the case, is to set aside everything in the pursuit of truth. My job is to present the facts to the grand jury, and the grand jury applies those facts to law," the attorney general of Kentucky said. "If we simply act on emotion or outrage, there is no justice. Mob justice is not justice. It just becomes revenge."

The city settled a wrongful death lawsuit of $12 million with the Taylor family but did not confess to wrongdoing.

Kenosha, a city of approximately one hundred thousand people north of Milwaukee, Wisconsin, experienced similar violence in the police shooting of Jacob Blake. In addition to inflicting millions of dollars of destruction downtown, rioters blocked the interstate highway.

According to police, the father of six was undeterred by a Taser and displayed a knife prior to being shot outside a girlfriend's home. Officers had been dispatched because the woman complained that Blake trespassed on the property even though she had a restraining order against him. Blake had been arrested the previous month for third-degree sexual assault, trespassing, and disorderly conduct.

After a thorough investigation, the Kenosha district attorney declined to file charges. Blake suffered paralysis from the waist down in the shooting.

The crescendo of violence seemingly went unabated in Kenosha when Kyle Rittenhouse, whose social media posts supposedly indicated pro-police, "Blue Lives Matter" sentiments, fatally shot two members of a large mob that was chasing him down the street. Rittenhouse fell to the ground in the pursuit, somersaulted, and came up firing his AR-15 assault rifle. The seventeen-year-old Rittenhouse said he was in the neighborhood to protect a car lot from looting. He faces homicide and reckless endangerment charges.

Local officials worried there could be violence on presidential election day because of the contentious political and societal environment, but the nine polling places in Wicomico County reported nothing more than harmless banter. Lewis stepped up security nonetheless: "It's all-hands-on-deck with our agency and all of our allied agencies, just to ensure that it is a smooth process," he said.

"It's always better to be safe than sorry," concurred a resident. "I just think with the way things are going today, it's best to be safe."

The drum roll to diminish law enforcement presence by defunding the police has arguably been loudest in the Pacific Northwest.

Carmen Best, the first female African American police chief in Seattle, was assailed for allowing her officers to dispense tear gas at rioters who were ransacking the city after George Floyd died.

When the city council voted to cut her pay, slash the department's budget by $4 million, and eliminate up to one hundred officers, she was outraged. "This is not about the money, and it certainly isn't about the circumstances. I have a lot thicker skin than that. It is about the overarching lack of respect for the officers. Targeting my command staff and their pay—it just felt very vindictive and punitive, and I don't want them to be affected by that type of animus."

Protesters, many of them masked Antifa and BLM anarchists dressed in black, even marched to her house. Best, who grew up in nearby Tacoma, Washington, was a twenty-eight-year veteran of the Seattle Police Department.

"It's tragic when we are in a society where they allow hoodlums and thugs to chase people out of a city and order law enforcement to stay out of the 'free zone,'" Lewis said.

The obsession with "defunding" and "reimagining" the police found traction in the CHOP (Capitol Hill Organized Protest) quadrant of downtown Seattle that attracted an odd array of anarchists, protesters, homeless, and mentally challenged people living in tents.

An art gallery and garden created initial appeal. Official police presence was scant within the relatively autonomous six-square-block radius. One resident admitted, "The CHOP was really good for a week. The last two weeks, it turned into a militant cult."

The realities of survival began to crystallize as a modest number of individuals actually held regular jobs and bought supplies. They had contended that uniformed police officers should not answer calls concerning mental illness, homelessness, and poverty, but there were limited resources and alternatives. The experiment spiraled out of control, with two fatal shootings of African Americans, precisely the people protesters allegedly wanted to liberate from police oppression.

Assumptions that the riots would halt upon Donald Trump's ouster and the election of Joe Biden were waylaid the night of his inauguration with vandalism and intimidation in Denver, Sacramento, Seattle, and Portland, Oregon, where windows were broken at the local Democrat party headquarters and the Immigration and Customs Enforcement (ICE) building.

"Very weak, very weak," is how Seattle community activist Victoria Beach characterized the city's response to the violence. After the mayor's office bemoaned "threats, vandalizing, and misogynistic and homophobic hate speech" as unacceptable, Beach said: "We're not talking about all that other stuff. We are talking about these fools who are nightly destroying our city."

Once again, the narrative was caught in the crosshairs of political correctness and diabolical devastation.

"He (Sheriff Lewis) is tough but fair. His presence can be intimidating—but that's not a bad attribute," said a Frederick Avenue resident thankful to be in Wicomico County at the zenith of the rioting. "No pandering to a specific group because it is PC."

Not far away from Seattle is the state capital of Olympia, where Evergreen State University police were told by the school president to "stand down" as a mob of two hundred "social justice" students cursed and confronted Professor Bret Weinstein for questioning the merits of an edict to ban all white people from campus for a day. Weinstein and his wife, a faculty colleague, received a settlement after resigning; the school's white female police chief quit her job and sued Evergreen for creating a hostile, racist working environment.

Three hours south of Seattle lies Portland, known for lush green spaces, refried hippies, "Keep Portland Weird" signs, and most recently, a community under siege.

Antifa, sardonically termed "anti-fascist fascists" by adversaries, is based in Portland and was instrumental in the rioting that occurred for months in 2020.

Stacey Gibson boarded up her Subway franchise in total disgust. "I mean, they (elected officials) say a lot of things but actions are what matters. They don't prosecute anybody. They'll arrest them, but they'll be out in a few hours. I don't have any idea why they don't, you know, just crack down on it."

"Everyone else has opinions about law enforcement, but we aren't supposed to defend what we do," Lewis said. "I've been in law enforcement thirty-seven years and you don't let the prisoners run the prisons."

Juggling the wishes of rattled residents and venomous demands for social justice, Mayor Ted Wheeler battled defiantly with President Trump, rejecting federal assets as government buildings and police precincts were being overwhelmed in 2020. Feeling the heat from Antifa and BLM, the city also admonished Police Chief Jami Resch for enlisting an all-white command staff.

Ridiculed for permitting the use of tear gas to repel rioters early on, the embattled mayor banned its essentially potent "CS" ingredient. "His decision hurts community safety and impacts officer safety," asserted Daryl Turner, president of the Portland police officers' union.

Protesters staged a "sit-in" in the lobby of the mayor's condominium building, then ordered him to resign on his fifty-eighth birthday unless he agreed to cut police funding by one-half. When he ventured to explain himself outside the federal courthouse, they screamed like a pack of hyenas, splashed paint, and chased him back to his office.

Tensions worsened in August 2020 when Antifa insurrectionist Forest Reinoehl fatally shot counter-protester Aaron Danielson. Authorities killed Reinoehl a short time later.

There is now a larger, more ruinous sector in Portland than Seattle, with unsanitary conditions, vandalism, structural damage, and homelessness so wretched that it has been likened to a "third-world city" slum. Heavily-armed, ruthless Antifa bullies "patrol" the area on motorcycles as police are directed by city hall to recede.

The same "Day of Rage" that Antifans crashed statues of Teddy Roosevelt and Abraham Lincoln, they shot holes in the front window of Heroes American Café owned by a black military veteran, saying he wrongly donated revenue to police organizations.

"They have no idea what a police state is. We are blessed to live in this country. We are imperfect, but we are by far the best country in the world," Lewis said, mentioning that millions of people want to move here.

Mayor Wheeler won a competitive race for re-election over "progressive" candidate Sarah Iannarone, a devout supporter of Antifa.

Within a few months, Wheeler tempered his sniveling submission to the anarchists by requesting $2 million in law enforcement funding that had previously been depleted. Antifa rewarded him with more rioting, torching American flags and the federal facility.

"There is just too much blood on the streets. We have got to be determined; we have got to be fed up about (the violence) and want to do something about it," exhorted Portland pastor Ed Williams because of the burgeoning crime rate.

Wheeler and Portland languished in the lunacy of "revolutionaries" like Darby Marshall Howard, arrested twice in a matter of hours. Accompanied by several dozen Antifa goons, he first punched a television in the lobby of the Wells Fargo Center, the city's tallest building, and kicked an automatic sliding door, causing more than $1,000 damage. Not satiated, he then struck a police officer in the head. Donning tattoos of a knife, crosses, a spider, and barbed wire, he was jailed momentarily, returning the same evening to slam a scooter into the courthouse, wearing the neon orange shoes he had been issued earlier by authorities.

Sheriff Lewis's leadership is steadfast for Wicomico County residents, observing the pandemonium and liquidation of law enforcement in other areas of the United States. "Because of who he is—his character, personality, value system—he refused to compromise quality delivery of public safety to the citizens of the county," Maciarello said. "This is probably the least talked about aspect of the job, but his capacity for advocacy for the sheriff's office (which was really advocacy for the citizens he was serving), was second to none."

Exemplifying pandering politicians and their sycophants' reluctance to challenge Antifans, Montana legislator Braxton Mitchell's proposed bill to designate them a terrorist organization met stiff resistance from legislators.

"The [Antifa] end goal is to abolish the US and overthrow the government," said Portland native, investigative journalist, and author Andy Ngo, who was severely beaten by the communist anarchists and fled to England as they threatened his life. "They have been given cover by the mainstream press and academe."

Ngo disagrees with FBI Director Christopher Wray's claim that Antifa is merely an ideology. According to Ngo, the decimation of local law enforcement is Antifa's immediate priority.

The liberal bastion of Asheville, North Carolina, slashed $770,000 from its law enforcement budget in September 2020. Republican lawmakers countered with the Police Funding Protection Act that would reduce state revenue for local jurisdictions cutting law enforcement funding by more than one percent. "We're seeing radical extremists launch vicious attacks on enforcing our laws right here in

North Carolina," Senator Chuck Edwards said.

"In an age of popular 'defund the police' and the attitude toward law enforcement, [Sheriff Lewis's] stance is needed. Otherwise, we would be a community without protection in our very homes," said Norma Dobrowolski of the University Neighborhood Association in Wicomico County. "Seeing Mike Lewis on television and radio interviews makes me think we are protected by a strong figure. I am heartened that the sheriff will uphold the Constitution and not waiver to popular undermining of law and order and our values as a country."

Early retirement, sudden resignations, and extended medical leave dropped nearly two hundred officers from the Minneapolis Police Department following George Floyd's death, but citizen complaints about slow response time and escalation of crime in the city could not be squelched.

In February 2021, the Minneapolis city council unanimously approved $6.4 million of additional funding for police. The mayor pledged to bring in recruits with academic majors in social work, psychology, and criminology, and those volunteering in programs such as the Police Activities League. Three council members favored establishing a public safety department blending social services with police as debates germane to law enforcement raged on.

In March, a lengthy *New York Times* article "Minneapolis residents in tug of war over policing ten months after George Floyd Death" reported violent crime surging by 66% in urban neighborhoods and shooting victims being dragged to ambulances because of barricades in an "autonomous zone" obstructing deployment of police and emergency response personnel. It preyed predictably upon the racial dichotomy: "Residents all over town complain of officers using excessive force, like a recent confrontation in which a white officer appeared to wind up and punch a Black teenager."

A smattering of groups, such as Voices of Black Mothers United, a subset of the nonprofit Woodson Center in Washington, D.C., take exception to howls and cries for defunding. Members have lost their own children to inner-city violence.

"Despite the fact that over 80% of black people want police to spend the same amount of or more time in their community, a radical fringe of people who will not have to deal with the consequences are trying to 'defund the Police'—and claim this is what people in dangerous neighborhoods want," founder Robert Woodson said. "That simply is not true. We've heard enough from them. Now is the time to listen to the actual neighborhoods and people who suffer as violent crime spikes."

According to columnist Tom Elias of the *Deseret Sun,* city and county officials in California have put Asians at risk by delivering the defunding police platform of Black Lives Matter: "The spate of anti-Asian violence in communities as disparate as Sacramento, San Jose, Los Angeles, San Leandro, and Orange County dramatically shows this was folly. All this has documented that even the 'model' minority known for high achievement and founding large and successful businesses of many types can suddenly be targeted."

The duress and vacillations afflicting law enforcement are clearly emblematic of something more colossal and sinister. People have called the Maryland Eastern Shore "a bubble" for its isolation and resilience, but Wicomico County Sheriff Mike Lewis recognizes that the national narrative wields repercussions for his agency and the place he grew up.

"Law enforcement is being challenged every step of the way right now. If you don't like your interaction with the police, obey the law," he warned. "Most law enforcement officers I have known are trustworthy, and I know how we should treat people."

CHAPTER FIVE

SECURING SOVEREIGNTY AND THE
SECOND AMENDMENT

Needless to say, Lewis was happy to learn that Yvette Herrell, a Republican US Representative from New Mexico, and Arkansas Senator Tom Cotton were introducing the "Defending Our Defenders Act" designating the murder of a federal, state, or local law enforcement officer a federal crime warranting the death penalty or life in prison. The killer's affiliation with anarchist groups, an intentional ambush, and prior threats against police would influence the level of punishment.

"Criminals who cut short the lives of our brave officers should be met with the fiercest penalties," Cotton said. "Killing a police officer not only ends a precious human life—it's also an assault against the safety of every American who lives in the community that officer protects."

With law enforcement officers occupying the wheelhouse of their scorn, conspirators in the left-wing subterfuge accusing the country of a racist, sexist, homophobic, and xenophobic legacy have clashed with Americans branded as incurably fascist, racist

"Trumpers" determined to preserve their archaically patriarchal way of life.

Conservatives abhor radical Democrats for inciting an Antonio Gramsci cultural agenda, broader than traditional Marxism, to infiltrate "hegemonic" institutions such as media, colleges and universities, organized religion, corporations, and government through divisive identity politics, "check-the-box" intersectionalism, and critical race theory coalescing around contempt for white privilege, especially white males.

"The interpretation of the world through the lens of 'social justice,' 'identity group politics,' and 'intersectionalism' is probably the most audacious and comprehensive effort since the end of the Cold War to create a new ideology," said British author and journalist Douglas Murray.

According to Sheriff Lewis, "Our beliefs, our opinions, are being abolished every day by the cancel culture movement that has enveloped the United States."

"Identities" pertaining to race, gender, sexual preference, and other supposedly oppressed groups are more relevant, the narrative espouses, than simply being an American. People have been submerged in a cage match between capitalism and looming full-blown "utopian" socialism as the waters of the insidious, insular "deep state" flow murkier and deeper than virtually anyone fathomed.

Murray said "anti-racism" that defines "an entire group of people, their attitudes, pitfalls, and moral associations, based solely on their racial characteristics is itself a fairly good demonstration of racism. For 'whiteness' to be 'problematized,' white people must be shown to be a problem. And not only on some academic, abstract level but in the practical day-to-day business of judging other people."

College campuses, Salisbury University included, are flooded with race-based curriculums, safe spaces, and institutional equity divisions evolving from critical race theory, viewing "Western, capitalist societies as systemically evil and tainted, and in need of systemic revolution," Cornell University law professor William Jacobson said.

With freedom of expression and divergent perspectives imperiled in the academy, Jacobson dovetailed that "there is a clear distinction between trying to expand the pool of applicants (in diversity initiatives) to ensure equal and fair treatment of all without regard to race, which is the goal of the Civil Rights Movement, and the coercive political movements of so-called 'anti-racism' activism which have little to do with equality."

Wall Street Journal columnist Charles Lipson noticed the "buzzword" politically correct semantics transitioning from "quotas" and "affirmative action" to "equity" favoring equal outcomes over identical opportunities. "Only a powerful central government could impose the intensive—and expensive—programs of social intervention. Only an intrusive bureaucracy could specify rules for every business, public institution, and civic organization. Isn't equity just a brand name for the oldest program of achieving equal outcomes? Its name is socialism."

Sheriff Lewis's contempt for political correctness and its allegories radiates from a written mantra in his office: "Political correctness is a doctrine fostered by a delusional, illogical minority and promoted by mainstream media, which holds forth the proposition that it is entirely possible to pick up a piece of shit by the clean end."

Coca-Cola and other corporate giants now mandate racial sensitivity training designed by social justice warriors such as Robin DiAngelo, the author of *White Fragility* who says whites being nice to black people only emboldens "racial disparities" through condescension. In DiAngelo's mind, her course confronts racism and unconscious bias to forge an inclusive workplace. "It's a process that needs to involve people of color, and that needs to go on as long as your company is in business."

"We've challenged our Diversity and Inclusion Council, as well as our associates, to put forth suggestions we can put into action to ensure our associates, especially our associates of color, feel safe, valued, and equal," said Kathryn Danko, chief diversity officer at Perdue Farms.

Three-term US Republican Congressman Jason Chaffetz of Utah said the Democrat party decided "that to save democracy, they must subvert it. To protect free speech, they must silence it. To fend off fascism, they must practice it. To promote good public policy, they must resist it. In the end, it appears to uphold the rule of law, some felt they must violate it," adding that crusading for exclusive control produces "a long list of institutions politicized, weaponized, or otherwise sacrificed in a progressive power grab."

Representative Sean Patrick Maloney, a Democrat from New York, unapologetically said recent bills by the party "don't have anything to do with socialism or defunding police," deviously retreating from the rapacious narrative and urban carnage condoned when it came to vanquishing Trump, Republicans, and anyone else with unpleasant perspectives.

When asked what Trump's opponent in 2016, Hillary Clinton, meant by "deplorables" Lewis pointed at himself, paused, and said, "Anyone who voted for Trump."

There was fervent supposition, but no confirmation from law enforcement, that bricks, bottles, Molotov cocktails, and makeshift weapons wielded by rioters in 2020 were supplied by billionaire George Soros and wealthy sympathizers desiring a borderless, global "reset" to exterminate Western civilization. As it turned out, COVID-19 likely accelerated the agenda along with critical race theory deeming white privilege the original sin.

A recall campaign was started in March 2021 against Los Angeles County District Attorney George Gascon, a criminal justice "reformer" who accepted $2.5 million from Soros in his election campaign. A "Victims Vigil" was held to inaugurate the petition for his removal. The aggrieved say Gascon champions early release of rapists, arsonists, drive-by shooters, assailants with deadly weapons, hostage-takers, and traffickers of minors for sexual exploitation.

The protests and riots at the U.S. Capitol in January 2021 cemented the polarization of the nation as legislators attempted to certify electoral votes rendering Biden victorious in a corrosively disputed election. While arrests were made of bona fide Trump loyalists, video surveillance recorded five buses of Antifa members, some of whom allegedly instigated and participated in the mayhem.

"The Capitol Police clearly underestimated what the event was going to be—the nature of the crowd—and made no plans to collaborate, seek additional assistance, until the crowd showed up at their front doorstep. And then it was too late," said William Bratton, who was police chief in Boston, New York City, and Los Angeles.

Millions of Trump supporters were labeled "scum" and satanic "cult" extremists who richly deserved "reprogramming," harkening the allegation years before that his adherents had been "body-snatched" and wired by aliens in reference to the 1956 horror movie.

Alexandria Ocasio-Cortez (AOC), a US representative from New York, categorized all Republicans as "white supremacists."

Wicomico County Sheriff Mike Lewis, unbeknownst to anyone but a few insiders for security reasons, navigated the arrest by the FBI of Kevin and Hunter Seefried, Wicomico County natives who moved to Laurel, Delaware. The family duo had made national news for accessing the Capitol building waving a Confederate flag. Son Hunter allegedly broke out a window to gain entry.

Through various sources, Lewis learned that Kevin Seefried only felt safe surrendering to him. "He knew they were the most wanted men in America. He was afraid the FBI would kick down their door and frighten his grandchildren."

Sure enough, when Lewis arrived to meet Kevin and Hunter at his office, four FBI agents were waiting outside. The sheriff allowed them to bid several family and friends farewell before relinquishing the suspects to the feds.

Both men were charged with entering a restricted building, violent entry on Capitol grounds, and disorderly conduct. Hunter was also charged with destroying government property.

"I do not think for a minute that anyone went over there to overthrow our government," contended Lewis. "A group of proud patriots went, believing the election was stolen not just from President Trump but from them."

Lewis said that some of the president's comments emboldened them to let their voices be heard at the Capitol building. "Once they saw how little security there was there, they moved in closer," Lewis said with the caveat that Antifa heavily infiltrated the protest and conceivably led the charge onto the premises.

He emphasized, however, that anyone perpetrating assaults, property damage, and physical intimidation of the governmental process must be held accountable and prosecuted to the fullest extent of the law.

"And so should all of the Antifa and Black Lives Matter people protesting violently in this country unmolested and unabated after rioting and assaulting cops the last six years. The actions at the capitol pale in comparison," Lewis said.

Derek Chauvin's murder and manslaughter convictions in the death of George Floyd momentarily averted worse rioting in April 2021, with the trials of three other police officers at the scene slated for late summer.

The mother of law enforcement officer Brian Sicknick, who died in the melee at the capitol, said a stroke took his life rather than the fire extinguisher reputedly brandished by Trumpers in *New York Times* and liberal media portrayals. Of the other four fatalities, two succumbed to medical conditions, one was trampled by the protesters, and one—namely, Ashli Babbitt—was shot in the neck by police.

A professed Antifa and Black Lives Matter associate, John Sullivan, was arrested for engaging in the capitol building onslaught, reportedly selling video he recorded at the scene to CNN and NBC News for $70,000.

> "Progressive leftist elitists have bought social media, alphabet networks, and run the biggest corporations. They control the narrative and are running the country their way now. They have the Oval Office, the House, and the Senate. The America we've known all our lives is hanging on by a thread," injected a reader of the daily online publication *Epoch Times*, a robust outpost of conservatism.
>
> *www.theepochtimes.com*

Lewis bashed the national media's willingness to ignore atrocities committed by BLM and Antifa, and the "damn fools" brainwashed by the toxic, unfettered rhetoric. "They (the media) are extremely leftleaning, and they are fanning the narrative embraced overwhelmingly by the left. I don't think they will ever come back to a more reasonable approach to informing the American people in a balanced and ethical way. They need a total makeover. Even Fox News has been turning the other way."

"The threat to free speech actually comes from the likes of left leaning cultural, educational, and media sectors," Chaffetz said. "Technology giants like Twitter, Facebook, YouTube, Google, and even PayPal have gotten in on the censorship game—where errors or overreach almost inevitably fall to the benefit of leftist speech."

House Democrats wrote letters to AT&T, Amazon, Verizon, Apple, Comcast, Dish Network, and other carriers, imploring them to "deplatform" Fox News, Newsmax, and One American News for alleged misinformation about the Capitol breach and COVID-19 pandemic— yet another assault on the First Amendment.

"Right now, I am afraid we are imploding," Lewis asserted. "We are destroying ourselves."

Senator Marsha Blackburn, a Republican from Tennessee, likened the silencing of conservative voices with the Chinese: "China is trying to cancel the United States of America. China and Big Tech . . . they have a crazy relationship. They have been allowing the Chinese Party to spew all of their information. Conform or they will cancel you. Sounds a lot like Communist China, doesn't it?"

Harry Potter, numerous classic Disney productions, Dr. Seuss, Eminem to a nominal extent, J.K. Rowling for allegedly unfavorable comments regarding transgender people, and actress Jodie Comer because of her rumored conservative boyfriend are among the legions of people in every walk of life hunted by the social justice warriors.

Cancel culture, with roots in political correctness reviled by Sheriff Lewis, is described as "the phenomenon of promoting the 'canceling' of people, brands, and even shows and movies due to what some consider to be problematic remarks and ideologies."

Indeed, Abraham Lincoln was surely ruminating about the trappings of the First Amendment and free expression when he said, "Don't interfere with anything in our Constitution. That must be maintained, for it is the only safeguard of our liberties."

"Whoever would overthrow the liberty of a nation must begin by subduing freeness of speech," Benjamin Franklin said.

The reality television show *COPS*, first aired in the 1980s and is regarded by Lewis as a refreshingly accurate portrayal of police work. It, too, had been the victim of pernicious cancel culture in the entertainment media. Lewis said *COPS*, along with the highly similar *Live PD* and *Live PD: Wanted* were taken off the air shortly after George Floyd's death.

Live PD had asked him for permission to film the travails and adventures of the Wicomico County Sheriff's Office for a year, but Lewis declined, knowing that constantly having camera crews in their midst would be a burden to his officers—not to mention the possibility that one misstep could enrage the anti-police cabal.

His instincts did not betray him. Williamson County, Texas, has been sued for its connection with *Live PD*. One suspect alleged he suffered a broken shoulder because his arrest was delayed and sensationalized for the camera crew. He claimed to have warned deputies of his mental health issues and suffered a heart attack. According to the lawsuit, "[The sheriff] created a culture around the show that rewarded escalation of conflict and violence."

COPS, transmitted by FOX with the disclaimer "filmed on location with the men and women of law enforcement. All suspects are innocent until proven guilty in a court of law," premiered in Fort Lauderdale and Brevard County, Florida. Sheriff Nick Navarro earned a reputation for interdicting the drug trade of billionaire Pablo Escobar and other kingpins, preceding Lewis's gambits years later.

Lyrics of the "Bad Boys" theme song by Inner Circle from the *COPS* series supposedly offended the fragility of political correctness while extrapolating the "enforcement" aspect of policing that marginalizes wayward people who made self-inflicted wrong choices:

> Bad boys, whatcha gonna do
> When Sheriff John Brown come for you

Tell me, whatcha gonna do when they come for you

When you were eight and you had bad traits

You go to school and learn the golden rule

So why are you acting like a bloody fool?

If you get hot, you must get cool

You chuck it on your mother, you chuck it on your father

You chuck it on your brother, you chuck it on your sister

Nobody naw give you no break

Police naw give you no break Soldier naw give you no break Why did you have to act so mean?

Don't you know you're a human being?

Born with a mother and the love of a father

Bad boys, bad boys, whatcha gonna do

Whatcha gonna do when they come for you?

The line "Born with a mother and the love of a father" sadly alludes to many of today's juvenile delinquents and adult criminals who grow up fatherless.

Sheriff Clarke delineated the dilemma: "Imagine you were a single mom getting benefits from the federal government. You'd get more money by being single than by having a husband who managed to hold down a job. The liberal War on Poverty (waged by Democrat President Lyndon Johnson) turned out to be basically a declaration of war on the black family. As the government expanded, it gave handouts that discouraged self-improvement, employment, and marriage."

Also holding Hollywood accountable for societal ills, Lewis recalled the movie *The Mule* directed by one of his favorite actors, Clint

Eastwood, that stereotypically depicted vicious, corrupt southern police brutalizing an elderly man who was running cocaine for a Mexican drug cartel. "It tore my heart out. They paint us with a broad brush."

Eastwood glamorized and eulogized plenty of firearms while playing cops during his career on the silver screen, earning himself and Hollywood hundreds of millions of dollars as Dirty Harry, uttering "make my day" and reaffirming the vigilante recourse of god-fearing Americans against the tidal wave of lawlessness. Gun sales in the United States have skyrocketed concurrently with urban crime rates in the wake of social volatility, political instability, personal uncertainty, and mutual animosity that frightens citizens who have never armed themselves before.

To say that Wicomico County Sheriff Mike Lewis is an ardent proponent of the Second Amendment in the Bill of Rights of the US Constitution is probably an understatement. In fact, he argues that the disparity between the timid outcry over attacks on freedom of expression exalted in the First Amendment and the relentless assault on the Second Amendment is extreme.

The telling passage of the Second Amendment reads that "a wellregulated militia, being necessary to the security of a free State, the right of the people to bear Arms, shall not be infringed."

Lewis sparred often with Maryland Senator Jamie Raskin over legislation proposed to dilute gun rights. Raskin, now a member of the US Congress, unleashed ugly tangents and was the chief architect of the rebuffed second initiative to impeach President Trump.

James Madison, considered the most influential framer of the Constitution, wrote how the government's standing army would be unlikely to conquer the empowered militia, invoking European kingdoms that were "afraid to trust the people with arms" and that the "existence of subordinate (local) governments forms a barrier against the enterprises of ambition."

Those words rang loudly for Lewis when, in 2014, he forecasted rebellion waged by his constituents should the federal government implement measures to deprive Americans of their freedom under the Second Amendment.

"Our culture is to hunt and fish. We love our way of life down here, and it's a simplistic way of life," the agitated sheriff said. "I can tell you this: if [the feds] attempt to strip our citizens of their right to bear arms, there will be an all-out civil war."

Lewis said lawful people must be able to defend themselves, their homes, and property with firearms, particularly in more rural settings. "There are locations that could take ten or fifteen minutes for law enforcement to respond."

He is convinced that people, not guns, ultimately kill. In his estimation, the "bad guys" will always enjoy access to weapons, meaning stringent gun control leaves mainstream Americans at a dangerous disadvantage that's only been exacerbated by the conniving impetus to defund local law enforcement and the politically defiled nationwide crime rampage in the summer of 2020.

Anticipating a heavily-armed drug den that year, Wicomico County sheriff's deputies searched a property in Delmar. Records show cocaine, crack, Ecstasy pills, marijuana, and $10,000 cash were seized from the premises. Deputies reported that twenty-three-year-old Shyheim Mitchell threw a loaded AK-47 out a back window of the house as the search progressed. They also found a Tak MK rifle with sixteen rounds in the magazine and a "drum" style magazine containing 9 mm bullets.

Deputies arrested Mitchell, Syncere Pinkett, nineteen, and Jasmine Banks, twenty-four. Charges for possession of narcotics with intent to distribute and possession of firearms were levied.

Dorchester County Sheriff James Phillips hailed the DOJ's Project Safe Neighborhoods program "as an example of what an investigation can accomplish when all allied agencies come together" following the conviction of a Salisbury man for possession of stolen firearms.

Attempting to hide his identity in a hoodie, mask, and gloves, Ricky Sanabria pilfered twenty-seven weapons from a gun store in Federalsburg, a few miles north of Wicomico County. He was arrested on the lam in Nebraska and sentenced to five years in federal prison.

Stolen firearms were discovered at his Salisbury residence and his parents' Hebron home. The Wicomico County Sheriff's Office was familiar with Sanabria, whose exploits prompted agents from ATF (Alcohol, Tobacco, Firearms, and Explosives) to join the probe.

In another case consummated by the DOJ's Project Safe Neighborhoods initiative, information gleaned by the Wicomico County Sheriff's Office prompted the arrest of convicted felon Jeffrey Dean Lecates, fifty-two, for gun trafficking and illegal possession of ammunition. Authorities executed a search warrant of his Salisbury home, which turned up a bevy of incriminating evidence.

The distinction between recidivistic criminals and law-abiding citizens possessing firearms is important, according to Lewis. Delaware Senator Brian Pettyjohn was charged with attempting to bring a weapon on a commercial aircraft after TSA security retrieved a loaded handgun from his carry-on bag.

In a plea deal, the felony charge was dismissed and probation of eighteen months resulted from having a concealed handgun on his person, a misdemeanor.

"In the absence of a criminal record, individuals arrested for handgun offenses such as this one involving Senator Pettyjohn are normally released on their own recognizance. He was detained long enough to interview him about the crime, conduct the appropriate background investigation to make certain he was not prohibited from possessing a firearm, that there were no open protective/peace orders against him, and to confirm his itinerary," Lewis explained. "He normally carries his weapon for self-protection, and was negligent in not removing the weapon from his carry-on bag."

Shortly after his election, President Biden proposed measures that would essentially deem millions of gun owners criminals, a number inflated by Americans purchasing firearms at a record pace because of the riots and lawlessness around the country.

The US Concealed Carry Association recoiled from Biden, saying "[We] exist to help amid danger, save lives, and keep our families safe, and we believe our leaders in Washington have an incredible obligation to pursue these goals."

The noose around gun racks tightened in March 2021 when the House of Representatives passed two bills drastically expanding background checks for firearms purchases. Eight Republicans voted with partisan Democrat members.

Representative Ben Cline, a Republican from Virginia, was not among them: "I will not stand by and allow our rights to be stripped away. My colleagues on the other side of the aisle claim that these bills save lives. However, nothing in them would have stopped any of the recent mass casualty shootings that have occurred in our country."

Lewis testified against the state's Firearms Safety Act prior to its ratification in 2013. One of the strictest gun laws in the nation, the act requires firearms applicants to supply fingerprints and complete training for obtaining a handgun license online. It bans fortyfive types of firearms, limits magazine capacity, and outlaws gun ownership for people committed involuntarily to mental health facilities.

Lewis said his opposition prompted a deluge of emails, handwritten letters, phone calls, and office visits from people supporting the sanctity of the Second Amendment. He started keeping a binder in his office of salutary notes—laminated, of course. "Those (sheriffs) in the rural areas all felt the way I did," Lewis recalled. "State police and the highway patrol get their orders from the governor. I get my orders from the citizens of this county."

He hosted a special town meeting on gun control that attracted Congressman Andy Harris, a number of sheriffs from the region, and State's Attorney Maciarello, who called the event "cathartic."

Lewis reassured the audience that "I don't aspire to be a delegate. I don't aspire to be a senator. I aspire to be sheriff."

"Well, Mike, if you plan on continuing to be my first and last defense against tyranny and supporting my right to keep and bear arms against the overreaching arm of the state, brother, you've got my vote. One less office for the local Republicans to worry about," expressed a blogger who attended.

"Many of these gun laws make future victims for these criminals who continue to steal, rob, rape, and murder while holding an illegally obtained firearm to their neighbor's head. We need to strengthen criminal penalties for those convicted felons found committing a crime with a firearm. We already have excellent gun laws on the books that carry serious penalties for those violating these laws. Until we have truth in sentencing, we will continue to re-arrest those criminals determined to be a menace to society," said the sheriff with a parting shot at the porous criminal justice system.

Wicomico EXILE, a subset of Maryland EXILE, rigidly targets fugitives, suspects with criminal records, and convicted drug offenders in firearms possession and commission of crimes. Sixteen-year-olds face adult prison time for using a firearm to perpetrate a crime or illegally carrying a gun. The program focuses on coordinated state and federal prosecution, the proactive pursuit of violent recidivistic criminals and gangs, stopping illicit firearms trafficking, information sharing among law enforcement agencies to locate armed felons, and public awareness.

According to sheriff's office records, forty-six-year-old Melvin Wolinski of Eden was charged by deputies with possession of a shotgun by a disqualified person and possession of ammunition while being a prohibited person, having fired a shotgun behind his home on Skylar Drive. Prior criminal convictions in Wicomico and St. Mary's counties enabled his arrest.

Sheriff Lewis's bold rhetoric echoed in the last three years as he and pro-gun rights advocates successfully repelled legislation in the state of Maryland to further regulate "long gun" (rifle and shotgun) transfers, imposing burdensome background checks, licensing, and potential confiscation. Violations, according to provisions in the legislation, could have resulted in five years behind bars and fines amounting to $10,000.

"The way the bill is written, it is impossible to comply in Wicomico County," Lewis huffed. "I can't send my deputies on a suicide mission. Sending police to take guns away will likely cause citizens to shoot at law enforcement officers."

Widespread seizures of long guns, he posited, would deviate significantly from "red flag" cases when a judge signs an extreme risk protective order, requiring a citizen to relinquish his or her weapons and ammunition.

Sheriff Lewis and Maryland Republican Delegate Mike Smiegel, representing the northernmost Eastern Shore, collaborated on a video for public and legislative consumption detailing concealed carry provisions and stressing that openly carrying a long gun down the street is unlawful. When he was criticized for enlisting sheriff's personnel and equipment to craft the piece, Lewis said, "We use our resources every day to produce public service announcements. It is also my job as sheriff of Wicomico County to educate the citizens on what the law is, and I am proud to have taken part in that."

He said lawmakers who generate gun control legislation are frequently ignorant about firearms: "They have no idea about the difference between a long gun and a handgun. Many of them have admittedly never fired a weapon in their lives."

Lewis said detractors of his refusal to comply were hypocrites, recalling Baltimore state's attorney Marilyn Mosby's "renegade" decision not to prosecute marijuana possession cases.

Johnny Mautz, a Republican delegate from Talbot County on the Eastern Shore, weighed in: "There are some people here (in the capital) who just don't like guns. I don't think their issue is with background checks as it is with the Second Amendment."

"If the [long gun bill] passes, we will not comply in Wicomico

County. Law-abiding citizens are being penalized because of Baltimore City's inability to control their crime. And I'm sorry— I'm not someone's puppet," said Lewis before the legislation was defeated. "They (the legislators) keep pushing and pushing. If Maryland lawmakers had their way, they would take away our Second Amendment rights."

The sheriff receives daily updates on shootings that happen around Maryland. "You always see 'nothing to report' in the eastern region, in the northern region, in the western region. But the Baltimore central region? Homicide after homicide after homicide."

Lewis said he is willing to be unelected and to stand up for what he feels is right. "Some sheriffs aren't as vocal as I am, but I've had enough. Other sheriffs have had enough. I am going to stand up for not just the citizens of Wicomico County but citizens across the state of Maryland and citizens across the United States of America."

The words of President Ronald Reagan echoed resoundingly: "Evil is powerless if the good are unafraid."

Someone asked Ben Franklin, "What kind of government have you given us?" as he was exiting Independence Hall. "A republic, if you can keep it!" Franklin responded.

Fueled by his public crusade ostracizing "tyrannical" state and federal government, Lewis proposed that a "symbolic but meaningful" Second Amendment Sanctuary, later referred to as Second Amendment Preservation County, be adopted in Wicomico. Similar resolutions have been passed by the Maryland counties of Harford, Carroll, and Washington, and North Hampton and Accomack counties on the Virginia Eastern Shore.

Lewis told the council that "making a statement" is important. "It is an equalizer for the weak and a neutralizer against the strong."

The autonomy of Wicomico County was ostensibly preserved in the proclamation's three central pledges to:

1. Not tax firearms, accessories, or ammunition not common to other goods and services;
2. Not maintain independent registration or tracking of firearms; and
3. Not impose independent measures for confiscation of firearms, accessories, and ammunition from citizens.

Restrictions ratified by the Maryland General Assembly were declared "unconstitutional" in the document.

National disturbances, in concert with local concerns, undermined the momentum of Lewis's plan. He requested that the council "delay the resolution indefinitely," citing emails, phone calls, anecdotal feedback on the street, meetings with residents, trepidation lodged by the NAACP, and the distraction of COVID-19.

"The county is hurting," Lewis admitted. "Now is not the time (to broach the proposal)."

The developments sparked tangible worry and resentment on social media:

> "I'm sure he has his reasons, but just so he knows, we will not back down. When it goes full throttle it will be game on."
>
> "Salisbury, the new Baltimore."
>
> "If you are not proficient in weaponry, take time to do so that you can protect your family and property. Don't be concerned with legality, be concerned with survival."
>
> "Smart thing to do right now. Just delay."
>
> "Well. Time for a new sheriff."
>
> "Mike Lewis, stand your ground and don't back down. We elected you because you're tough. We already have a mayor and a police chief who have their heads all up the lefties' asses. We need a NAAWP (National Association for the Advancement of White People). Wait, blacks will riot and claim racism if we did that. Double standard."
>
> "Waiting for cooler heads to prevail is a smart move. Most are running on emotions right now that could work against his suggestions for a sanctuary county. I'm sure Mike knew he'd take flak over this, but it was a better play at this point in time. RESPECT for understanding the mood and situation."
>
> "You all wanted law enforcement to step back, folks. Well, you got it, and it is only going to get worse. Criminals don't stop being criminals while cops are being reformed."
>
> "Mike, remember when you were an MSP and had the highest arrest rate for drug trafficking in the state? That's the Mike Lewis we need now."
>
> *sbynews.blogspot.com*

Lewis read the resolution at a council meeting in early 2021 without an official vote, emitting confidence it would pass by 2022.

"We'll be moving forward in the very near future. Timing is everything. We need this today more than ever."

"The role of the sheriff is to be an interposer between the law and the citizen. Sheriffs do have the power to nullify or ignore, a law if it is unconstitutional," said Maryland Delegate Don Dwyer, a Republican from Anne Arundel County. He added that James Madison referred to nullification as a rightful remedy of the Constitution and that the Second Amendment forays of Lewis and other sheriffs in Annapolis are "bold."

The National Rifle Association (NRA), Oath Keepers, and the Constitutional Sheriffs and Peacekeepers Association (CSPA) are among the gun advocacy groups bolstered by Lewis.

The NRA labeled a pro-gun control organization's petition to revoke the sheriff's Maryland police training certification "pathetic" in the aftermath of his comment about "civil war" should the federal government meddle with the fundamental right of Wicomico County citizens to bear arms.

Lewis called the petition "ludicrous," saying "they're going to twist and turn this to suit their own special needs. I will continue to identify and arrest all criminals who violate the law."

The sheriff supports Oath Keepers, an organization with forty thousand members in forty-eight states that extols the unification of veterans, law enforcement officers, and first responders to "defend the Constitution against all enemies, foreign and domestic."

"I studied what the Founding Fathers meant about the Second Amendment, the right to keep and bear arms, and the conclusion is inescapable," said Richard Mack, former sheriff of rural Graham

County in Arizona and founder of CSPA. "There's no way around it. Gun control in America is against the law."

Another Arizona sheriff of like mind, Pinal County's Mark Lamb, was a keynote speaker for the 2020 Lincoln Day Dinner arranged by Lewis at the Black Diamond Lodge in Fruitland. Lamb, described as "passionate about defending our freedoms, constitutional rights, and the American way of life" by Lewis, hosted *Live PD: Wanted*, which solicited public assistance in tracking down dangerous felons.

Lewis and Lamb have become good friends over the years. During one of our interviews in his office, the sheriff unveiled a cowboy hat Lamb gave him that would have authenticated Deputy Sheriff Wyatt Earp at the O.K. Corral shootout in Tombstone, Arizona Territory.

Most of the nation's 3,080 sheriffs are more outspoken than police chiefs because they have been elected, not appointed. Lewis's unique persona and the relative independence of the position synthesize productively.

His quest to preserve the Second Amendment and protect Wicomico County from intrusive government evokes salutations in cyberspace from Americans across the country:

> "As for Sheriff Lewis, I defend his comment (about civil war if they try to take our guns away). This is part of his sworn duty, and to exercise free speech to demonstrate his resolve to the people who elected him is reassuring. I feel a good sheriff is the last defense against our tyrannical government."
>
> "I am staying in MD at the moment, and I found the Sheriff's
>
> Facebook page and sent him a message encouraging him to 'stick to his guns' on this issue. Look at Switzerland, where all citizens must be

in their army, keep firearms, and receive regular refresher training. One of the SUPER low crime rates in the world."

"Sheriffs are the only elected officials that are independent of the federal and state governments. They report to 'We the

People' of the US Constitution. Stand with our honest and

Constitutionalist sheriff."

"Give this sheriff a promotion for his courage and honesty! God knows Washington DC politics could use a healthy dose of his medicine. He is spot on with the civil war if big brother comes for our weapons. God forbid it comes to that. Give me liberty or give me death!"

"I remember the name USSR, Union of Soviet Socialist Republics and the DEMOCRAT SOCIALIST parties that existed to overthrow free men and women and move them to slavery. Now we have the Socialist Democratic Party in Washington. They tell us we are too ignorant to lead ourselves and they are the only ones smart enough—and they have failed miserably."

"We need more state and local law enforcement to stand with the people. Kudos for resisting the tyranny of the federal government."

Patriot Headquarters Blog

Lewis is on the advisory board of the new Protect America Now organization that was developed with the motto "Together We Will Stand Against Lawlessness." Along with Lamb and sheriffs from Virginia, Illinois, Florida, Massachusetts, and Missouri, the group aspires to protect the Constitution and the Second Amendment, contest massive illegal immigration, and neutralize government bloat and higher taxes portending socialism.

Lewis became one of more than two hundred sheriffs petitioning President Biden to secure the southern border. "It absolutely terrifies me—it terrifies me for our country's future, it terrifies me as a citizen of Maryland—because these drug traffickers are well-entrenched in Maryland today."

"Mike Lewis is truly one of the most honorable, dedicated, and courageous leaders I have been humbled to work with over the years," Senator Carozza said. "His servant leadership has benefitted the people of Wicomico County, the State of Maryland, and the United States of America."

As the virus surged and other crises crippled the nation in 2020, he enthusiastically committed to vying for Wicomico County sheriff a fifth time in 2022. "I love my job," Lewis said, reneging on a pledge to wife Denise many years earlier to hold office only two terms.

"Even though I've been very blessed to run unopposed, and it is a Herculean effort to run this county as sheriff, make no mistake: if there is anyone that truly believes they can do a better job I will help them prepare their campaign," said the sheriff with characteristic confidence and zeal.

The confluence of tirades and initiatives to defund the police and disarm law-abiding citizens casts a foreboding shadow that renders Americans susceptible to suffocating socialism and totalitarianism, in Lewis's opinion.

"Not on my watch in Wicomico County," assured the sheriff, who refuses to capitulate. "I was elected as a law-and-order-sheriff, and that won't change."

Haven P. Simmons

EPILOGUE

This book engages three major themes to inform and entertain the reader, the most obvious of which follows the genesis, ambitions, and accomplishments of the person, Wicomico County Sheriff Mike Lewis. It is no accident that Lewis has garnered a statewide, regional, and national profile in criminal justice circles that reverberates from his pride in the community, the sheriff's office, and law enforcement. The second theme endeavors to educate the reader through the lens of Sheriff Lewis's story about what the policing profession actually entails. Hopefully the book provides the reader with broader knowledge of law enforcement obligations beyond negative media portrayals, the controversial but mesmerizing enforcement role, and the rare, sometimes annoying encounters most law-abiding citizens experience with cops. Augmented by the sheriff's desire to preserve the Constitution and repel cancel culture, the final theme paints the big picture of government and the greater society that places local law enforcement in a crucial, albeit vulnerable and often underappreciated position. Demands for defunding municipal, county, and state police agencies by anarchists and political parasites harboring oligarchical, global designs should terrify Americans accustomed to dedicated law enforcement leaders emulating the same standards as Sheriff Mike Lewis.

ABOUT THE AUTHOR

Haven P. Simmons worked in and around the media fifteen years for daily newspapers, ABC television affiliates, and as a government spokesman representing the mayor and police department in Bradenton, Florida. He first developed interest in law enforcement covering the criminal justice beat for the Sarasota, Florida, *Journal* and *Herald-Tribune*. He has taught media relations and public information at the Federal Emergency Management Agency (FEMA) and the National Fire Academy, and was an observer-controller for the Texas A&M Engineering Extension Service (TEEX). He retired as a communication professor from Salisbury University in Maryland. Dr. Simmons earned Ph.D. and M.A. degrees from the School of Journalism and Mass Communication at the University of Iowa. His dissertation and related publications study the relationship of media, law enforcement, and government; he most recently coauthored *Police, Politics, and the Press: A Florida Case Study*, with veteran detective Patrick Proudler in 2020.

ACKNOWLEDGEMENTS

I am immensely grateful to Wicomico County Sheriff Mike Lewis for permitting me to write our book. The task was highly rewarding because of his cooperation, charisma, congeniality, achievements, and riveting perspectives that resonate with the author. I knew Mike was a popular and highly effective sheriff already, but his animated speaking to my Media and Criminal Justice class at Salisbury University on several occasions manifested an energetic, irrepressible force of nature warranting greater exploration. Too many Americans are complacent, timid, and frightened these days. I respect Sheriff Lewis profoundly as a beacon of sensibility and courage against the ominous factions that conspire to eviscerate our government and way of life envisioned by the Founding Fathers in the United States Constitution.

REFERENCES

McFadden, R. Whitman Dismisses State Police Chief for Race Remarks. *New York Times.* (1999, March 1). https//www.nytimes.com

Trinko. T. Why Liberals Identify with Criminals. American Thinker. (2015, October 31). https//www.americanthinker.com.articles

Multijurisdictional Counterdrug Task Force Interdiction Introduction. YouTube. (2007, August 30).

Jacobs, E. Ted Cruz among GOP lawmakers slamming Biden as border crisis escalates. *New York Post.* (2021, March 10). https//nypost.com

Hanson, V.D. *The Case for Trump.* Hatchett Book Group (2019).

BBC. MS-13: The story behind one of the world's most brutal street gangs. (2017, April 19). https//www.bbc.com/news-world-us-canada-39645640

Delmarva Now. Sheriff Lewis: Trump's border wall essential to stop illegal drugs. (2019, August 16). https//delmarvanow.com/story/opinion

WGMD. Wicomico County Sheriff speaks out against bill to make Maryland a sanctuary state. (2020, February 16). https//www.wgmd.com/wicomico-county-sheriff

Parsons, K. 71 Suspected Drug Dealers Indicted in Wicomico County. WBOC. (2012, December 20)

https//www.wboc.com/story/203928895

Factbase. Donald Trump Vetoes Resolution Blocking Emergency
Border Declaration. Website. (2019, March 15).
https//factbase.se/transcript/donald-trump-remarks

The Federal Bureau of Investigation Baltimore Division. Member of
Salisbury Drug Organization Sentenced to 10 Years in Prison. Website.
(2011, July 15). https//www.fbi.gov/baltimore/press-releases

Akins, S., & Mosher, C. Oregon Just Decriminalized All Drugs—Here's
Why Voters Passed This Groundbreaking Reform. *U.S. News & World
Report.* (2020, December 10). https//www.com/news/best-
states/articles

Capital News Service. Marijuana Legalization Proposed in Maryland
Legislature. WBOC. (2021, February 23).
https//www.newsbreak.com/news/217358872931

Thompson, A. Fentanyl Now Mixed With Crack Cocaine and Ecstasy,
Causing Local Spike in Overdoses. Cincinnati Public Radio. (2019, May
3). https//www.wvxu.org/post

U.S. Food and Drug Administration (FDA). FDA launches public
education campaign to encourage safe removal of unused opioid pain
medicines from homes. (2019, April 25). https//www.fda.gov/news-
events/press announcements

Hooper, B. Concerns Raised Over Proposed Marijuana Law Changes.
The Dispatch. (2020, February 20). https//mdcoastdispatch.com

Scott, R. A Historical Perspective of the Office of Sheriff. National
Sheriffs' Association. Website. www.sheriffs.org/about-

nsa/history/roots

Goldberg, J. The Color of Suspicion. *New York Times Magazine.* (1999, June 20). https//www.newyorktimes.com

Bassett, G. Sheriff Mike Lewis is building a strong force, Pac 14 One on One. (2019, February 21). https//salisburyindependent.net/independent-qa

The Dispatch. Wicomico Deputy Cleared in Fatal Shooting Case; Officer's Reaction Deemed 'Reasonable.' (2015, December 30). https//mdcoastdispatch.com

Fernandez, Camilia. Police ask for public's help in solving cold case homicide. WMDT. (2020, July 29). https//wmdt.com

WBOC. Deputy Recounts Being Shot, Speaks Out About Disability Benefits. (2012, April 14). https//www.wboc.com/story/173377391/deputy-funk

Delmarva Now. Wicomico deputies reach collective bargaining agreement. (2016, April 6). https//delmarvanow.com/story/news/local

Badcock, Merris. MD Sheriff: Four state is a 'target enriched environment' for drug trafficking. WDVM. (2016, January 12). https//www.localdvm.com/news/md-sheriff-four

Wicomico County Sheriff's Office. Bay to Beach. (2021, February 15). https//www.facebook.com/wicomico sheriff

WBOC. Sheriff Lewis Tells Us What to Do When Getting Stopped by Police. YouTube. (2016, July 25).

Wicomico County Sheriff's Office. (2021, January) https//www.facebook.com/wicomicosheriff

Wicomico County Sheriff's Office. (2018, May)https.www.facebook.com/wicomicosheriff

Daily Mail. The farm of horrors: Maryland sheriff discovers 25 dead horses who were so desperate for food they ate aluminum siding off a house. (2018, March 18). https//www.dailymail.com.uk/news/article-5515427

Ash, S. Breaking: Eden Puppy Mill defendant takes plea deal. WMDT. (2019, October 7). https//www.wmdt.com

Hooper, B. Wicomico 'In Dire Need' of Deputies. *The Dispatch.* (2019, May 23). https//mdcoastdispatch.com

The Dispatch. Wicomico Sheriff's Deputies Honored with Awards. (2013, March 14). mdcoastdispatch.com

Live PD. Julie Brewington transport. YouTube. (2018, September 19).

WITN. Update: Kenansville man wanted in fatal shooting arrested in Maryland. (2019, June 15). https//www.witn.com/content/news

Green, S. State's Attorney Rematch Heats Up. *The Dispatch.* (2010, September 30). https//www.mdcoastdispatch.com

Hahn, J. Wash. High School Gives Band Students Individual Bubbles to Curb Covid Spread in Viral Video. *People.* (2021, February 25). https//people.com/human interest

Parra, E. Cop expert defends shooting of man in wheelchair. Wilmington *News Journal.* (2015, October 2). https//www.usatoday.com/story/news/nation-now

FindLaw. Marcus Bounds v. Deputy Benjamin Parsons Corporal Cristan Taylor Officer Keith Heacock Officer Traavis Dallam. Web site.

(2017, July 14). https//caselaw/findlaw.com/us-4th-circuit/1868015.html

WBOC. Updated: Salisbury Man Held Without Bond in PNC Bank Robbery. (2019, August 23). https//www.wboc.com/story

Associated Press. 'This is not a car show:' Over 100 people arrested during H2oi car rally in Ocean City. WJLA (2020, September 28). https//wjla.com/news/local/police-arrest-dozens

Junkin, V. Blurred Boundaries. *Daily Times.* (2014, April 7). https//www.delmarvanow.com/story

Rule, K. Edwin Fletcher sentenced to 30 years for assault of three officers. WMDT. (2014, December 18). https//www.wmdt.com

Wainman, Laura. Salisbury University closed Thursday after racist graffiti discovered, FBI investigates. WUSA. (2020, February 19). https//www,wusa9.com/article/news/education

WBOC. Suspect Identified in Racist Graffiti at Salisbury University. (2020, February 21). https//www.wboc.com/story

Post News. Hate crime hoax: African American pleads guilty to defacing university with racist graffiti. (2020, June 22). https//postnews2.blogspot.com

Associated Press. Maryland man pleads guilty to hate crime connected to racist graffiti found at Salisbury University. *Baltimore Sun.* (2019, March 31). https//www.baltimoresun.com

Richardson, B. Students quizzed on 'Pyramid of White Supremacy' at Salisbury University in Maryland. *Washington Times.* (2018, January 18). https//www.washintontimes.com/news

Shaw, J. Why I Left 'Racially Hostile' Smith College. Triggernometry. YouTube. (2021, March 3).

Rectenwald, M. *Springtime for Snowflakes: Social Justice and Its Postmodern Parentage.* (2018, New England Review Press).

Anderson, M. When Schooling Meets Policing. *The Atlantic.* (2015, September 21). https//www.theatlantic.com/education/archive

Corley, C. President Johnson's Crime Commission Report, 50 Years Later. NPR. (2017, October 6). www.npr.org

Chapman, S. Invisible Cops. *Slate.* (2001, November 12). https//slate.com/news-and-politics

Cann, B. The Bloods (1972-). Blackpast. https//www.blackpast.org/african-american-history/bloods-1972

WBOC. Salisbury University Student Charged with Soliciting Child Pornography. (2020, September 22). https//www.wboc.com/story

FindLaw. By and Through v. Wicomico County Sheriff's Department. (2018, February 12). https//caselaw.findlaw.com/us-4thcircuit/1889050.html

Tron, G. Resource Officer's Quick Response Stopped Maryland Shooter. Oxygen. (2018, March 21). https//oxygen.com/crime-time/resource-officer

FBI (Federal Bureau of Investigation). Baltimore TTP Bloods Leader who Produced "Stop Snitching" Video and Eastern Shore TTP Leader Convicted of Racketeering. FBI. (2010, January 20). httsp//archives/fbi.gov/archives/baltimore/press releases

Gates, D. Hurt bald eagle rescued by Wicomico deputies. Delmarva

now. (2016, September 16).
https//www.delmarvanow.com/story/news/local

True Crime Daily. Sarah Foxwell Case: Abducted girl's brave little sister helps track down killer. (2017, September 18).
https//truecrimedaily,com/videos/0-944un6gn

Wicomico County Sheriff's Office. Christmas Angel. (2020, December 25). https//www.facebook.com/wicomicosheriff

WMDT. Update: Former martial arts instructor sentenced for sex abuse of minor. (2017, November). https//www.wmdt.com

Junkin, V. Man argues with judge during sentencing. Delmarva Now. (2013, December 20). https//delmarvanow.com/story/news

McManus, B. Blame only the man who tragically tried to resist. *New York Post*. (2014, December 4). httsp/www.nypost.com

Police1. NYPD Cop Killer: "I'm Putting Wings on Pigs Today." (2014, December 20). https//www.police1.com/ambush/articles/nypd-cop

Eastern Shore Criminal Justice Academy. Wor-Wic Community College. Website.

Jackman, T. Who wants to be a police officer? Job applications plummet at most U.S. departments. *Washington Post*. (2018, December 4). httsp//www.washingtonpost.com/crime-law

CBS Baltimore. Maryland Senate Passes Police Reform, Transparency Measures, Including Anton's Law. (2021, March 3).
https//baltimore.cbslocal.com

Mac Donald, H. *The War on Cops*. (2017, Encounter Books).

Reyes, K. An Open Letter to Everyone Who Hates Cops. *Law*

Enforcement Today. (2019, March 21)
https//www.lawenforcementtoday.com/open-letter

Clarke, D. *Cop Under Fire.* (2017, Worthy Books).

Halpern, Jake. The Cop. *The New Yorker.* (2015, August 3).
https//newyorker.com/magazine

Smith, M. How the Eric Garner Case Decision Compares with Other
cases. *New York Times.* (2019, July 16). https//www.nytimes.com

Celona, L., Cohen, S., Schram, J., Jamieson, A., & Italiano, L. Gunman
executes 2 NYPD cops in Garner 'revenge.' *New York Post.* (2014,
December 20). https//nypost.com

Jamieson, A., & Bailey, C. 6 Officers Shot in Florida and Pennsylvania,
2 Killed and 4 Wounded. NBC News. (2017, August 9).
https//www.nbcnews.com/news/usnews

Baxter, E. Dallas Shooting is Deadliest Attack on Police Since 9/11.
Hill Country News. (2016, July 8). https//texashillcountry.com/dallas-
shooting-deadliest-attack-since-9/11

Madhani, A. Several big U.S. cities see homicide rates surge. *USA Today.*
(2015, July 10). https//www.usatoday.com/story/news

Clarke, D. *Cop Under Fire.* (2017, Worthy Books).

Waters, Barbara. Remarks Made Public Service to All Difficult.
Delmarva Now. (2016, July 19).
https//delmarvanow.com/story/opinion/readers

Mooney, Thomas. Defending Sheriff Lewis After Attacks. Delmarva
Now. (2016, July 19). https//delmarvanow.com/story/opinion/readers

McCarthy, A. Understating Black-on-Black Murders. *National Review.*

(2020, June 25). https//www.nationalreview.com

Loury, G. We're Playing with Fire. Triggernometry. YouTube. (2021, February 14).

Mac Donald, H. *The War on Cops*. (2017, Encounter Books).

Adams, M. Nobody Wants to Be a Police Officer Anymore. Brobible. (2018, December 5). https//brobible.com/culture/article

Justia Law. Leftridge v. Matthews. (2013, September 30). https//lawjustia.com/cases/federal/appellate

Police Magazine. Ice Cream Makers Launch Campaign to Make It Easier to Sue Police. (2021, January 27). https//www.policemag/592426

Mac Donald, H. *The War on Cops*. (2017, Encounter Books).

Nuzback, Kara. David Watson sentenced to more than 100 years. *Cape Gazette*. (2013, November 22). https//www.capegazette.com/node/57053

Pollitt, R. What we know about the assault of a Delmar police officer. Salisbury *Daily Times*. (2021, April 26). https//www.delmarvanow.com/delaware

Fox News. Hannity: Violence in Baltimore. (2015, May 27).

WBAL. Man Sentenced On Gun Charges After Taking Advantage Of Post-Riot Tension. (2015, December 14). https//www.baltimoresun.com

Mac Donald, H. *The War on Cops*. (2017, Encounter Books).

Junkin, V. Mike Lewis enters national stage with recent appearances. Delmarva Now. (2015, June 5).

https//www.delmarvanow.com/story/news/local

Daily Times. Cartoon. (2014, August 14).
https//www.delmarvanow.com

Hammit, D. Breaking out . . . Why I quit my job as a police officer and I'm not looking back. *Law Enforcement Today.* (2018, April 4). https//www.lawenforcementtoday.com/breaking

Simmons, H.P., & Proudler, P.J. *Police, Politics, and the Press: A Florida Case Study.* (2020, Copworld Press).

Newsmax. New Biden Executive Order Increases Voting and Voter Registration for Criminals in Prison and on Probation. (2021, March 8). https//www.newsmax.com/headline/criminal-voting

KVUE. Houston police chief blames Democrats' loss on Austin City Council members. (2020, November 4). httsp//www.kvue.com/article/news/politics/vote

Willis, M. Beat to Beat. United States Deputy Sheriffs' Association. Website. (2021, January).

Spiering, C. He Stands with Us, We Stand with Him—Police and Law Enforcement Officers Overwhelmingly Endorse Trump. Breithbart. (2020, September 9). https//www.breitbart.com/politics

Hanson, V.D. *The Case for Trump.* (Hatchett Book Group, 2019).

KSTP. Minneapolis police union releases letter criticizing city leaders; AFL-CIO, Education Minnesota call on him to resign. (2020, June 1). https//ktsp.com/news/Minneapolis-police-union

McCarthy, T. The celebrities who have given to the Black Lives Matter movement. Fox News. (2020, August 5).

httsp//www.foxnews.com/entertainment/celebrities

Bailey, A. Harry Styles Says He Stands In Solidarity With Black Lives Matter Protesters: Enough Is Enough. *Elle*. (2020, June 1). https//www.elle.com/culture/celebrities

Zuby. The Problem with Black Lives Matter. Triggernometry. YouTube. (2020, July).

Murica, L. VP candidate Kamala Harris chilling interview about BLM riots: 'They're not gonna stop. And they should not.' *Law Enforcement Today*. (2020, August 30). https//www.lawenforcementtoday.com/kamala-harris

McCarthy, T., & Moore, T. NYPD cops encouraged to 'strike' on July 4 to give its city 'independence.' *New York Post*. (2020, June 18). https//nypost.com

Moore, T., Celona, L., & Woods, A. Shootings surge in NYC amid disbanding of NYPD's plainclothes anti-crime unit. *New York Post*. (2020, June 19). https//nypost.com

Bredderman, W. De Blasio Defends Warning his Biracial Son About 'Dangers' of Police. Observer. (2016, February 18). https//observer.com

Reyner. S. Police Poll: 71 Percent of D.C. Police Force Might Resign. Newsmax. (2020, June 18). https//www.newsmax.com/politics/muriel-bowser

James, J. Mob Justice Is Not Justice: Cameron Defends Breonna Taylor Investigation. WUKY. (2020, September 23). https//www.wuky.org/post/mob-justice-not-justice

Wallace, D. Jacob Blake protests: Police hunt for suspect with long gun after 2 killed, 1 wounded in unrest. Fox News. (2020, August 26). https//www.foxnews.com/us/news/crime/police

WBOC. Wicomico County Sheriff's Office to Provide Security at Voting Centers. (2020, November 2). https//www.wboc.com/story/42855090

Kiefer, P.F. Police Chief Carmen Best Explains Her Decision to Resign; Durkan Says No Search for Replacement This Year. *South Seattle Emerald.* (2020, August 11). httsp//southseattleemerald.com

Choe, J. Residents demand answers from Seattle City Hall about ongoing protests. KOMO. (2021, January 21). https//komonews.com/news/local/residents-demand

CNN Wire. They envisioned a world without police. Inside Seattle's CHOP zone, protesters struggled to make it real. WHNT. (2020, July 5). https//whnt.com/news

Ailworth, E. Inauguration Day Protests in Portland, Seattle Turn Violent. *Wall Street Journal.* (2021, January 21). https//www.wsj.com/articles/inauguration-day-protests

Creitz, C. Portland business owner describes 'devastating' situation, says 'there are no consequences' for crimes. Fox News. (2020, July 29). https//www.foxnews.com/media/Portland-riots-out-of-hand

Bremner, S. Bret Weinstein and the cowardice of college leaders. *Spiked.* (2017, May 30). https//www.spiked.online.com

Post Millennial. Antifa rioters shoot through windows of veteran-owned café. Website. (2020, October 12).

https//thepostmillennial.com/antifa-rioters-shoot

Connelly, E. 22-year-old Portland protester arrested twice in the same day. *New York Post.* (2021, March 3). https//nypost.com

Blake, A. Montana bill to designate Antifa as a domestic terrorist organization group tabled in committee. *Washington Times.* (2021, February 27). https//www.washingtontimes.com.news

Miller, A. Portland mayor asks for additional police funding to address rising crime after slashing budget. *Washington Examiner.* (2021, March 13). https//www.washingtonexaminer.com/news/portland/additional-police-funding-rise-crime

Richardson, V. 'I am Antifa': Sarah Iannarone forces runoff in bid to become Portland's mayor. *Washington Times.* (2020, June 2). https//www.washingtontimes.com/news

CBS News. Suspect in killing of right-wing protester fatally shot during arrest. (2020, September). https//www.cbsnews.com/news

Ngo, A. Antifa Violence Won't Stop Under Biden. Triggernometry. YouTube. (2021, January 27).

Los Angeles Airport Peace Officers Association. It's Time for Americans to Face Reality. Website. (2020, September 16).

Edwards, C. Cities that 'defund police' would be punished under new NC bill. Website. (2021, February 15).

Navratil, L. Minneapolis to spend $6.4M to hire more police. *Star Tribune.* (2021, February 12). https//www.startribune.com

Eligon, J., & Arango, T. Minneapolis residents in tug of war over policing 10 months after George Floyd's Death. *New York Times.* (2021,

March 28). https//www.nytimes.com

Allen, V. Defunding Police Isn't Answer, Say Black Mothers of Slain Children. The Daily Signal. Website. (2021, February 2). https//www.dailysignal/defund-the-police-meaning

Elias, T. Asian violence shows folly of defunding. *Deseret News*. (2021, March 16). https//www.deseretsun/story/opinion

Pagones, S. Cotton, Herrell to introduce cop killer bills making it a federal crime to kill any law enforcement officer. Fox News. (2021, March 9). https//www.foxnews.com/us/republican-lawmakers

Thomas. B. Antonio Gramsci: The Godfather of Cultural Marxism. Foundation for Economic Education. (2019, March 31). https//www.fee.org/articles/antonio-gramsci-the-father-of-cultural-marxism

Murray. D. *The Madness of Crowds*. (2019, Bloomsbury Continuum).

Murray, D. *The Madness of Crowds*. (2019, Bloomsbury Continuum).

Eustachowich, L. New website tracks where critical race theory is taught in US schools. *New York Post*. (2021, February 5). https//nypost.com

Lipson, C. 'Equity' Is a Mandate to Discriminate. Wall Street Journal. (2021, March 4). https//www.wsj.com/articles/equity-is-a-mandate

Del Rio, M. Coca-Asks Its Workers to Be 'Less White" to Fight Racism. *Entrepreneur*. (2021, February 25). https//www.entrepreneur.com/article

Perdue Farms. A message from CEO Randy Day and COO Kathryn Danko regarding Perdue Farms' commitment to Diversity and

Inclusion. Website. (2020, June 3).

Chaffetz, J. *Power Grab*. (2019, HarperCollins)

Creitz, C. Ingraham: Leftist figures calling for Trump supporters to be 'deprogrammed' like Chinese dissidents. Fox News. (2021, January 13). https//www.foxnews.com

Stieber, Z. House Democrats' Attempt to Pressure TV Carriers Could Trigger Lawsuit: Dershowitz. *Epoch Times*. (2021, February 27). https//www.theepochtimes.com/house-democrats

Moore, M. Ex-NYPD Commissioner Bill Bratton calls for 9/11-like panel to probe Capitol riots. *New York Post*. (2021, January 10). httsp//www.newyorkpost.com

Din, B. DCCC Chair: Criticisms on socialism, defund the police are 'Republican caricature.' *Politico*. (2021, February 25). https//www.politico.com/news

Grimes, K. Recall Campaign Against Soros-Backed LA County District Attorney George Gascon. California Globe. Website. (2021, March 14). https//californiaglobe.com/section-2/recall

McDaniel, R., & Lanum, N. Ocasio-Cortez's 'white supremacist' accusations about Republicans 'reckless' and 'divisive.' Fox News. (2021, January 28). https//www.foxenews.com/politics/aoc-accusations

Chaffetz, J. *Power Grab*. (2019, HarperCollins).

Shiver, S. Capitol Police Officer Brian Sicknick's mom says he died of stroke, not a blow to the head. Blaze Media. (2021, February 23). https//www.theblaze.com

Romboy, D. Utah activist in Capital riot sold his video to CNN, NBC for $35k each, court doc says. *Deseret News*. (2021, February 17). https//www.deseret.com

Bowen, X. Big Tech 'Aiding" Beijing in Push for Global Dominance. *Epoch Times*. (2021, February 26). https//www.theepochtimes.com/big-tech-aiding

Kato, Brooke. What is cancel culture? Everything to know about the toxic online trend. *New York Post*. (2021, March 10). https//nypost.com/article/what-is-cancel-culture

Quotes by Abraham Lincoln. Abrahamlincolnonline.org

Goodreads. Ben Franklin Quotes. https//www.goodreads/com.quotes

Reding, S. Another Williamson County resident files lawsuit, saying broken shoulder from arrest sensationalized for 'Live PD." KVUE. (2021, January 26). https//www.kvue.com/article/news/investigations

James Madison Quotes—1788—Revolutionary War and Beyond. Jamesmadisonquotes.com.

Classic TV & Movie Hits. COPS. https//www.classictvhits.com/show.php?id=1038

Whitten, S. 'Cops' Canceled, 'Live PD' and 'Body Cam' shelved in the Wake of George Floyd Protests. CNBC. (2020, June 10). https//www.cnbc.com

Genius Lyrics. Inner Circle—Bad Boy Lyrics. Genius.com.

Clarke, D. *The War on Cops*. (2017, Worthy Books).

Hughes. S. Jamie Raskin Leads Democrats in Trump's Second Impeachment Trial. *Wall Street Journal*. (2021, February 7).

https//www.wsj.com/articles

Combs, H. Eastern Shore felon sentenced to five years in federal prison for illegal possession of stolen firearms. *Dorchester Star.* (2019, November 19). https//www.myeasternshoremd.com/Dorchester_star

U.S. Attorney's Office. Salisbury Felon Facing Federal Charges for Gun Trafficking and Possession of Ammunition. Website. (2021, March 26). https//www.justice.gov/usao/md/pr/salisbury-felon-facing-federal-charges

Goss, S. Delaware state senator gets probation in felony case. *News Journal.* (2017, September 29). https//www.delawareonline.com/story/news

Cowan, R. U.S. House passes two Democratic-backed gun control bills. Reuters. (2021, March 11). https//www.reuters.com/article/us-usa-congress-guns

Interactive Constitution. Right to Bear Arms. https//www.constitutioncenter.org

Bedard, P. Biden Gun Control would 'criminalize' 105m law-abiding people. *Washington Examiner.* (2021, February 23). https//www.washingtonexaminer.com/washington

Monoblogue. 2A town hall draws 500 citizens. Website. (2013, March 26).

Beeman, R. Perspectives on the Constitution: A Republic, if you can keep it. National Constitution Center. Website.

Bearing Arms. MD County Withdraws 2A 'Preservation' Resolution—Sheriff Says "Now Is Not the Time.' Website. (2020, June 16).

https/bearingarms.com/camedwards/

Junkin, V. Gun views spark effort to revoke certification. *USA Today.* (2014, October 7). https//www.delmarvanow.com/story/news/local

Johnson, T. NRA Goes to Bat for Sheriff Who Warned of Civil War with the Federal Government. Media Matters for America. Website. (2014, October 19).

Jackman, T. National Sheriffs' group opposed to federal laws, taxes, calls for defiance. *Washington Post.* (2016, April 18). https//www.washingtonpost.com/news/true-crime

Specter, C. House passes bill for tighter long guns regulation. *Dorchester Star.* (2020, February 7). https//www.myeasternshoremd.com/Dorchester_star

United States Department of Justice. Maryland Exile. https//www.justice.gov/usao-md-marylandexile

WBOC. Wicomico Sheriff, MD Delegate Appear in 'Open Carry' video. (2014, May 14). https//www.wboc.com/story/24975551

Police Tribune. Sheriffs Call Maryland's Proposed Gun Laws 'Suicide Mission.' (2019, March 1). https//policetribune.com/sheriffs-call

The Daily Ridge. Oath Keepers Seeking Additional Supporters and Volunteers for Relief Effort in Keys. Website. https//www.dailyridge.com

Goodreads. Ronald Reagan Quotes. Goodreads.com.

Proudler, P.J. *Cops and Robbers: Florida Police Chronicles.* (2021, Copworld Press).

Protect America Now. Website. https//protectamericanow.com

Sheriff Lewis smiles as he fields questions from the press during a candlelight vigil held in honor of those killed by illegal aliens. Washington D.C./September 2021

Sheriff Lewis holds a Second Generation Colt Python .357 Magnum recently released to the public. September 2021

Sheriff Lewis stands with Fox News host Will Cain along the Southwest Border wall in Cochise County, Arizona, just minutes after conducting an interview on Biden's border crisis. April 2021

Wicomico County Sheriff Mike Lewis and Sheriff Mark Lamb of Pinal County, Arizona, pledge to protect the Constitutional rights of their citizens, come hell or high water.

In 2006, then Maryland State Police Sergeant Mike Lewis poses with Troopers Dave McCarthy (L) and Mike Conner displaying twenty-two pounds of cocaine seized from the floor of a Chevy mini-van stopped on I-95 in Cecil County, Maryland. The cocaine, valued at just under $1 million, was found secreted within an after-market installed electronically controlled compartment.

Observing illegals as they move closer to the new border wall only hours before dozens of them torched through the structure, entered the United States, and were apprehended by sheriff's deputies. April 2021

Sheriff Lewis bonds with Colombian National Police "JUNGLA" Special Forces fighters following another mission into the Andes Mountains, 300 miles southeast of Bogota. 2014

Manning a door-mounted Gatling gun on a U.S. led fact-finding mission deep in the mountains of South America during a VIP tour by the Colombia National Police (CNP) traveling across the country via Black Hawk helicopters. (2014)

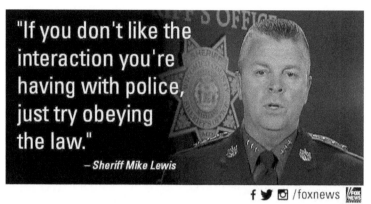

As riots besiege major cities, Sheriff Lewis's courageous candor goes viral, infuriating the anti-police cabal and earning the respect of law-abiding citizens.

Examining a clandestine lab seized by Colombian CNP forces, Sheriff Lewis holds up a kilogram of cocaine, among the many kilo presses and signature plates littering the operation just feet from the Amazon River in the far reaches of the Andes Mountains.

Sheriff Lewis with Mexican Federales providing security in Mexico City.

Heavily armed Mexican Marinas escort the U.S. delegation into the Sinaloa Valley where police discover a methamphetamine super lab.

Under the watchful eyes of a security detail in the Sinaloa Valley of Mexico, a Mexican Marina (Marine) poses with Sheriff Lewis while touring a crystal methamphetamine lab that was seized days earlier in Culiacan, home of Joaquin "El Chapo" Guzman, once the world's most powerful drug lord.

Sheriff Lewis graces the dining hall in the home of Mexico's U.S. Ambassador. (2019)

With indisputable Old West flair, Sheriff Lewis returns to Wicomico County from Tombstone, Arizona, where he met with a select group of sheriffs from across the nation to form a new Political Action Committee (PAC), a private-non-profit organization seeking to build a coalition of patriots determined to Protect America Now.

Mr. & Mrs. Sheriff Mike Lewis

Michael A. Lewis

SHERIFF

Wicomico County Sheriff's Office
401 Naylor Mill Road
Salisbury, MD 21801
(410) 548-4891

Sheriff Lewis and deputies display illegal drugs confiscated by the agency's
Community Action Team (CAT).

*Accompanying Florida Senator Marco Rubio, other dignitaries and law enforcement personnel to
surveil drug cartel operatives in Colombia. November 2014*

Sheriff Lewis and a dozen Wicomico County deputies deploy to guard city hall in 2015 with the agency's Mine-Resistant Ambush Protected (MRAP) vehicle designed to transport law enforcement assets, first responders, and victims of violence.

Interviewed frequently by FOX News over the years, Sheriff Lewis joins television icon Sean Hannity at the network's studios in New York City.

Greeting Donald Trump at the Salisbury Regional Airport and escorting the presidential candidate to a rally at Stephen Decatur High School. April 2016

Thumbs up with President Trump on border security and other favorable law enforcement developments during one of seven visits to the White House in eight months.

Revving but relaxing on one of his Harley-Davidson motorcycles.

Sheriff Lewis is the only American sheriff and the designated spokesman for an expedition of officials to Sinaloa, Mexico, sponsored by the U.S State Department.

He is flanked by female Sinaloa state police officers instrumental in discovering and dismantling equipment used to produce methamphetamine for illicit distribution in America.

Lewis kneels derisively at the temple dedicated to the late drug lord Jesus Malverde, a "Robin Hood" figure now revered by the cartels for supposedly providing them transcendently safe passage in and out of the United States.

CPSIA information can be obtained
at www.ICGtesting.com
Printed in the USA
BVHW041845230222
629950BV00013B/556